7 FIGURE FICTION

HOW TO USE UNIVERSAL FANTASY TO SELL YOUR BOOKS TO ANYONE

T. TAYLOR

PART ONE

HOW UNIVERSAL FANTASY SECRETLY CHANGED MY LIFE

**(AND MANY OTHERS')
WHILE CONFUSING
THE HECK OUT OF US**

AN INVITATION

**TO LEVEL UP
YOUR WRITING
AND MARKETING**
(if you're willing to open the gift)

CHAPTER ONE
HEYO!

My name is Theodora Taylor.

I'm an Amazon Top 10 Bestselling author of contemporary, sci-fi, and shifter romance. And…

That's it.

Seriously, that's it.

I don't have any superlatives above my name. USA Today or NYT Bestseller? Nope! As of this writing, I've never made a bestseller list outside of the Kindle store as Theodora Taylor. RWA Awards? Nada! I've never even applied.

**But I do make about
a quarter of a million dollars a year.**

To some writers, that's impressive.

To some, that's like, "Meh! I made that last February."

But I'm particularly proud of my annual $250K+ because I write what I want and whatever I want in a niche category called Interracial Romance (or IR as those of us who adore the category call it). My heroines are exclusively women of color, and some of my heroes are men of color too. On top of that, I do a lot of things that writers with good business sense don't…

1. I have no design background, but I've often insisted on making my own covers.
2. I write in a non-mainstream category.
3. And within that category, I hop genres: contemporary romance, bully, mafia, shifters, dark, aliens, romantic suspense…I do it all, often within the same series!
4. My original target audience is tiny compared to that of most romance writers.
5. I don't have a Facebook readers' group because I don't like commitment outside of marriage.
6. And as many of my readers can tell you, my themes, tropes, and steam levels are rarely consistent across my author brand.

Yet, I make what many would call a good living, and I've been fortunate enough to earn over seven figures in the last few years of my writing career.

I'm OBSESSED with crafting books so delicious and enthralling that tons of satisfied readers will catapult my earnings to 7 figures per year. That's why this book is called *7 Figure Fiction*.

It's a milestone. It's a target. It's a burning desire.

And if you're reading this book, I imagine you share my love of writing irresistible stories for voracious readers who can't wait to gobble up what you write.

But there's just one thing standing in your way: **You don't know if readers will love what you're writing.**

Let's note here that not all writers have this question. Many successful creatives craft stories for themselves without the worry of what their audiences will think. Good on them. Those authors should keep on trucking and do what they do best—nothing to see here.

This book is for the following type of writer:

THE NEWBIE: You're just starting out, and you have no idea if what you're writing will resonate with audiences. It's difficult, verging on paralyzing, to put words to paper because you feel so uncertain about whether your scenes and situations will hit the spot with potential readers. You fear that a poor launch with a poor reader response will discourage you from ever trying to write again.

THE GAMBLER: You've got a few books under your belt, and it STILL feels like you're rolling the dice every time you upload a book. Sometimes your new releases soar, and sometimes they belly-flop—not in a funny way, but with a hard, painful smack that leaves bruises and mental scars. You HATE not knowing which one it will be while you're crafting your novel.

THE ABANDONER: You're tip-tap-typing along on your work in progress when a pervading sense of doom stops your fingers in their tracks. SOMETHING IS WRONG with your book. You don't know what it is, but you sense something isn't quite jelling with the story's situations and/or characters. You've amassed a pile of unfinished drafts on your desktop that deserve to be finished. But you don't know how to proceed with that icky feeling in the pit of your stomach. Oh, the guilt!

THE BLANK: You've written yourself into a corner with a side character—a friend or a sibling of a character who deserves their own story. "When is X going to get their own book?" your readers demand. They hound you about this character's novel and post comments under every new release. But the thing is, you've got nothing. Oh, dear…

THE ENTERTAINER: Your main goal is to consistently write books that readers will ENJOY. The actual writing barely matters because it's about ENTERTAINING the reader. Perhaps you're transitioning from a career in an audience-obvious performing art like acting, music, or dramatic writing. So that old advice of "just write the book you want to read" doesn't do it for you. You want to KNOW that what you're writing will attract and *entertain* readers. You live for 5-star reviews and fan mail that lets you know your audience ADORED your book.

THE GRIZZLED HEART: you've written so many books that you've lost connection to the heart of a good novel. You've begun to feel like a hack, and you worry that you've lost your connection with your readers. You miss the original love you had for telling stories, and you long for your wide-eyed ingenue days like a former starlet yearns for her original youthful face underneath all that plastic surgery.

You know, my heart ached as I wrote out this list. Before I discovered the power of Universal Fantasy, I was each of these writers.

Now, I turn around novels in 4–6 weeks, but it took me *years* to write my first book because I was paralyzed by the fear of everyone hating it. And throughout my career, I've suffered through all the feelings listed above.

Until I discovered the one tool that helped me overcome the worst of my "will they like it?" anxieties, market my backlist books like a beast to readers outside my target audience, and double my income. Most importantly, this tool allowed me to craft irresistible books that delivered non-stop feels and thrills.

And that tool is **Universal Fantasy**.

If you're any (or many) of the above types of writers, think of this book as a gift. Inside, you will find a magic pair of glasses that will allow you to see the things you and others create in a new way.

These glasses will open your eyes to things you've never seen before in your own writing and help you market in a way that attracts readers who have never heard of you. After putting on these glasses, you'll also have a much easier time during the writing process.

But BE WARNED…

What is seen with these glasses can't be unseen. Once you discover the power of Universal Fantasy, you won't be able to undiscover it.

You'll see it everywhere, and you'll have trouble returning to your old, audience-disconnected way of writing and thoughtless consumption of entertainment.

Once known, Universal Fantasy will set up a permanent home in your head, always buzzing in the background.

You'll be able to ignore it—but you'll never be able to forget it.

So this is where you should stop reading if you're truly satisfied with your current writing life.

But if you're not afraid—if you're ready to know the secret hidden inside all bestselling stories, open the gift.

Keep reading…

CHAPTER TWO
WHAT IS HAPPENING?
WHY I GOT ANGRY—YES, ANGRY—THE FIRST TIME I MADE THE AMAZON TOP 100

So why was I so angry the first time one of my books made it into the Top 100 for the entire Kindle store? For the answer to that question, let's go back to me in 2011…

After stints as a playwright, radio writer, and women's fiction author, I'd basically become a "write-at-home mom" of one. And it wasn't going well.

My first women's fiction book, which had sold in a splashy deal, wasn't moving units to my publisher's expectations. Even worse, a potential movie offer for the novel had fallen through with the dissolution of Miramax.

My traditional publishing editor had just responded with a scathing email about the second novel I'd turned in as part of my two-book deal. Summary: she hated everything about the new novel except the quality sex scenes.

By this time, my original agent and I had fallen out. I'd managed to procure a new agent, and she'd agreed to start shopping my second book to other publishers, but who knew if anyone else would bite?

So, having earned zero dollars in new money that year, I found myself at a crossroads in my writing career.

I knew three things:

1. I could write quality sex scenes.
2. There was a reason the term "write-at-home mom" wasn't a thing. Because it was impossible. But I wasn't cut out to be a full-time stay-at-home mom. I absolutely hated it, and it felt like I was going out of my mind. And...
3. I needed to make at least $50K a year to put my child in daycare without feeling guilty about No. 2. That money would also allow our family a nice vacation or two in 2012.

Thus, I decided to give writing interracial romance as an indie writer a try. Why indie? To be honest, my experience with traditional publishing had left a bittersweet taste in my mouth. I didn't love having gatekeepers, and I was drawn to the freedom of managing myself and my own career.

Why IR? I chose this niche category because I was in an interracial relationship myself, and that had led to some interesting changes in my reading habits.

Before I married my white husband, I read romances featuring mostly either Black or white couples. Johanna Lindsey, Susan Elizabeth Phillips, Julie Garwood—those were my girls growing up. And as an English major at Smith College, I gobbled up books from Black romance publishing lines like Arabesque[1*] between all the required reading.

I gave up reading romances during my twenties, opting for more literary fare and women's fiction. But after my women's fiction career imploded and two brutal back-to-back miscarriages, I returned to books that celebrated love and happy endings. And I found myself wanting to read about women in relationships that looked like mine.

I was a voracious reader, but there wasn't much to offer in the category back then. Multicultural & Interracial Romance wasn't even a Romance subcategory in the Kindle Store at the time. So, when I decided to become an independent romance writer, I figured my potential readers were exactly like me—actively searching for books that reflected the kind of relationships we were in and hungry-verging-on-starving for romances that featured interracial couples.

I'd also read in some random place that according to the 2010 U.S. Census, intermarriage between husbands and wives of different races or ethnicities had risen 28% since 2000 to account for one in ten of all marriages. And according to one article I read on the subject, that number was expected to keep on rising into the foreseeable future.

So based on that gut feeling and a tidbit of research, I was like…

> **"Yes, IR is the best genre**
> **to invest in for me.**
> **I'll write what I want.**
> **Maybe I'll make my $50K.**
> **Yay! Let's do this."**

And I was right.

I surpassed my monetary goal in my first year of writing simply by writing within this niche category filled with voracious target readers.

From the start, I wrote IR and marketed heavily to IR audiences. I wanted Theodora Taylor to be synonymous with IR romance, so I created the IR Weekly Bestseller list to help my target audience find the multicultural books they were craving. I also went to romance conferences focused specifically on Black and interracial romance and got to know other readers who loved IR.

And, just like I hoped would happen, my target audience grew along with my sales.

But something interesting happened along the way to trying to reach every reader who wanted to read interracial romance.

I started attracting readers who WEREN'T in my original target audience.

First, it was Black women who weren't in interracial relationships.

Then it was white women who happened to find my books and liked them enough to read the rest of my backlist. And eventually, non-African American readers of color started reading my romances too. Those audiences grew along with my target audience and my sales.

Then, around 2015, I decided to become a six-figure writer…

Why?

Why not?

Other authors were making six figures a year. Why not me?

At first, I did this by simply writing more books…

MORE BOOKS!!!

These are the books I wrote the first year or so after deciding to become a six-figure writer. Please excuse these first effort and inconsistent covers. I just really want you to understand that I was NOT a marketing genius.

Main point: writing more books worked to some extent.

> **More books.**
> **More backlist.**
> **More sales.**
> **Yay!**

But then this frustrating thing kept happening…

Sometimes a book would flop, and I couldn't clearly state what had gone wrong. This was a real teeth grinder for me, as I consider myself a vessel for story. And it often feels like I've let down the characters who've chosen me as their writer when a book isn't well-received.[2*]

Before these launches, I was often plagued by a feeling that the disappointing seller just wasn't as good or appealing as other books I'd written. But I couldn't figure out why that was or how to fix it. The books that flopped often just felt…off.

I'm sure a few of you have had similar problems.

You're writing a book, and it's technically good. But for some reason, it just isn't sparking like you want it to if you're a new author—or like one of your more popular books if you've been at this a few years.

For quite a while, I tried fixing this occasional flop issue with craft.

I doubled down on three-act structure, started paying way more attention to GMC (Goal, Motivation, and Conflict), and outlined like a beast. I read craft books on writing—SO many craft books—and tried like hell to level mine up.

Sometimes that worked.

But sometimes, it didn't.

Sometimes I released a book with perfect structure, a great trope, and characters with clear GMCs. But I'd carry a bad feeling in my gut. I knew I'd tried my best, but for some reason I couldn't quite put my finger on, this book just wasn't going to spark as much love or sales as some of my not-as-technically-well-written bestsellers that had come before it. And that gut feeling was generally correct.

How did I deal with books that didn't live up to my sales goals?

Super simple, really. I'd lament for a couple days. Then I'd plop my butt down in my desk chair and work on the next thing. During breaks, I'd pray desperately to the writing gods that this next book wouldn't let down my story the way the last one had.

Sometimes the gods didn't answer.

And sometimes the opposite would happen…

**SURPRISE!
IT'S A FAN-FAVORITE BESTSELLER!**

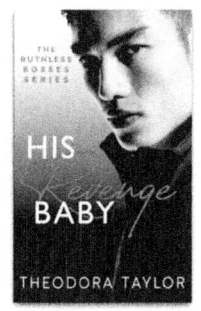

**Sometimes a book would become
a Kindle Store Top 100 bestseller,
and I had no idea why…**

I'll never forget the first time this happened in 2016—mainly because it was Super Bowl Sunday and Beyoncé would join Coldplay on stage for half-time—but also because *His Pretend Baby* became my first book to hit the overall Top 100 for the Kindle store.

To say I wasn't planning for this is an understatement. I'd written HPB as a sort of thought exercise novella on a long winter holidays road trip to visit my relatives in St. Louis and my in-laws in Dallas, Texas. I was shocked when the hero told me he was neurodivergent halfway through the trip, but I returned home with two things:

1. A lifelong desire to never road trip with three under-7 kids in the backseat again. (Seriously, don't do it!) AND…
2. A rough draft of a novella-length *something*.

The edit ended up taking me a whole week instead of the couple days I'd allotted for it. And it doubled in size. By the time I sent it off to my then-editor with a "fit this in whenever" note, I was seething that I'd let myself get derailed from my main goal, the last book in my fan-favorite Ruthless Russians series.

When I got it back, I threw it up on Amazon with a short pre-order and a hope and a prayer that it would earn me a few extra dollars toward my goal of becoming a six-figure author.

Imagine my surprise then when readers started messaging me and posting on my Facebook wall about how much they loved this book. Mothers of neurodivergent kids wrote me heartfelt comments and messages. Fans who'd been hounding me for the last book in the Russian series forgot all about Ivan and declared Go, the star of *His Pretend Baby*, was their new favorite book boyfriend. A 7-figure author duo I wouldn't have imagined even knew my name raved about the book to their readers. Most importantly…

It reached No. 69 in the Kindle Store

Not just in my IR category, but in the entire store!

And it completely ruined my Super Bowl Sunday.

My father, the teacher, loved to play the lotto. He did it pretty much every week of his life, starting from when it was a neighborhood game called "the numbers." He often dreamed out loud about what he'd do with the money if he won the Powerball.

My mother the accountant, on the other hand, advised us that he'd be better off investing that money in an interest-bearing savings account.

I'd assumed I was a dreamer like my father—I mean, c'mon, I'd grown up to become a full-time maker-upper of stories. But that Super Bowl Sunday, I discovered that I was indeed my mother's daughter. I fell into a depression over the next week and had a lot of trouble returning to my next book.

Though I was grateful for hitting the Amazon Top 100, it was a confusing and frustrating experience because I had no idea why readers responded to this book the way they did.

I needed explanations, receipts, numbers that added up. As it turned out, despite my decade-plus in California, I abhorred magic in a vacuum. I just couldn't take the blessing. Because if you don't know **WHY** your book becomes a bestseller… Arggh!!! It is SO frustrating!

Not knowing why means that you can't replicate that book's success. Not knowing why means you have to deal with the possibility that you might have magically written your best book and that everyone will hate what comes after. "One-hit wonder" is one of those phrases that sums it up perfectly for consumers but eats away at the hearts of creatives.

I would like to say I threw myself into trying to figure out my surprise bestsellers just as I did my surprise low sellers. It would be awesome to tell you I surveyed my readers, dug into my stats. Did everything I could to replicate those results.

But remember what I told you earlier about not always making great business decisions?

Instead, I decided these Amazon Top 100 books must be special snowflakes. I assumed there was no way I could replicate their success.

And I stewed in my frustration as I did the exact same thing I did when a book didn't sell. I moved on to the next book, and—Extra Anxiety Points—I now got to write the follow-up novel underneath a cloud of fear that this one wouldn't be as good as the one that came before it. The next books usually did fine—but seldom Top 100 awesome, which made writing the follow-up after a bestseller hit feel like a joyless grind.

Sadly, this "just write another book" anxiety cycle continued for years. Some new releases would become a mega success. And some terrifically written books would sink like a stone after a considerable release effort.

Even worse, I got stuck in a terrible habit of not putting a lot of effort into marketing a new release until I was sure that readers really liked it—either using sales or reviews as my measuring tape. This meant that I often lost precious opportunities to get the word out about the book during its first week of release.

It was so, so frustrating—not to mention a poor business strategy!

But then something fantastic happened.

I took a Facebook ads class.

"Wait, wait, wait," you're probably saying. *"How did an ads class transform you from an inconsistent writer to someone who almost always hits the Kindle Top 100 with every new release?"*

Well, two things became clear during that class.

At that time, and as far as I know now, my niche audience simply wasn't reachable the way Facebook ads are set up. While I could target a few television shows and movies featuring IR couples, there was no way to narrow down those results in meaningful ways. And there were no comparable IR authors on the FB targets list.

Simply put: I couldn't direct ads to my primary audience (readers who enjoy interracial romance novels) within the Facebook ads platform.

To be successful in this class, I could no longer just market to Black women who were actively looking for an interracial romance on Facebook. Even more challenging than that…I had to convince people outside of my niche audience, readers who'd never heard of me, that they wanted to gobble up my books.

In short, to take my sales to the next level, it was time to broaden my audience.

But how? How does a niche author garner wide appeal and make the hundreds of dollars she paid for that Facebook Ads class worth it?

The answer to that question is **Universal Fantasy**.

There are only, in my humble opinion, two kinds of readers.

> Readers who love your books.
> and…
> Readers who don't know they love your books yet.

But how do you reach those readers in the second category, no matter how scattered and inconsistent you are?

Again, the answer is…

Universal Fantasy

Universal Fantasy is why my sales tripled when I "accidentally" wrote three books that landed in the Amazon Top 100.

. . .

Universal Fantasy is why some authors get gobs of gushing reviews and some authors who write "way better" get crickets.

Universal Fantasy is the answer to many of the questions you might have thought were unanswerable or simply up to luck, like…

- Will this sell?
- Why is that selling?
- Why didn't this sell?
- Will readers like what I am writing?
- Why do I love the TV shows/books/entertainments I do?
- Why did I buy that thing I bought when I didn't intend to buy it?

Maybe you're like I used to be—anxious all the time. Scared that your bestselling books are flukes of luck and your worst-selling books are indicative of things to come.

Maybe you're just starting out and wondering how to turn occasional readers into rabid fans.

Maybe you've read a ton of writing books about structure and craft, but strangely, none of them actually talk about attracting and connecting with readers.

If so, keep reading to find out how to use **UNIVERSAL FANTASY** to write and market books that **SELL** to **ANYONE**.

---

1. * Arabesque was a publishing line owned by BET Books. While in college, I wrote and submitted a romance to them. They asked to see the full book, but eventually sent back a form rejection letter with a kind handwritten note that I should certainly try again at the bottom. I didn't. And Arabesque was eventually enveloped into Kimani after it was bought by Harlequin in 2005. After I became an indie writer, I did sign a two-book deal with Kimani. This made that dream come true…and taught me that I really preferred publishing as an indie writer.
2. *Heads up. I lived in California for almost two decades, so statements like these sound perfectly reasonable to me. Shoot me a message if you want to talk about crystals and tarot, too. Woo-woo all day, baby!

CHAPTER THREE
SO...WHAT IS UNIVERSAL FANTASY EXACTLY?

I'll admit that the definition of Universal Fantasy (UF) is hard to pin down—especially for me. Like most full-time genre writers, I used UF unconsciously for years without actually labeling it.

For much of my career, I vaguely thought of it as the reason(s) readers liked my books.

But if pressed to put an exact label on it now, I would say that Universal Fantasy is why readers *feel* things when they read my books—why they *connect with* and *enjoy* my books.

Let's take this concept back to the storytelling fires of our hunter-gatherer ancestors.

Perhaps one storyteller tells the true tale of how his older brother ate a piece of fruit that turned out to be poisonous while they were out foraging for food. The storyteller dragged his brother into a cave and stayed with him there overnight until he stopped throwing up and they could walk back to their group's temporary settlement.

That's a story, sure. It's got a beginning, a middle, and an end as well as an inciting incident, a climax, and a resolution. Great.

But how about if that storyteller told his story this way…

He and his older brother both wanted the same woman, but their father informed them the night before their planned forage that she would be given to the older brother simply because he was born first. While they were out in the wilds beyond their settlement, his older brother —who never listens to his weaker younger brother—ate a piece of fruit against his younger brother's advice.

A few shadow advancements of the sun later, his brother was puking and unable to walk. The storyteller realized the sun would go down soon, and his brother was too heavy for him to carry back to the settlement.

Thus, the storyteller walked away, leaving his brother to his fate, knowing that he would have the woman he wanted when he returned to their encampment. But then…

He spotted a cave just a few steps into his journey, and a voice inside of him told him he had to go back to save his brother. So he chose to return to his sibling's side and save him.

With great physical effort, he managed to drag his brother into a cave. They were safe. Or were they? After the sun set and they fell asleep, a low growl woke them from sleep. It was a predator!

The storyteller jumped to his feet, determined to save his brother.

I'll stop there and invite you to notice a few things:

1. That story was nearly four times as long as the original, BUT…
2. It was way more engaging and compelling.
3. You might even want to know what happens next! You could be wondering if the storyteller will get the woman in the end after he saves his brother.

That's because the second version of the story had all sorts of Universal Fantasies packed in: healing a family rivalry, saving a loved one from death, and pulling off heroic feats that prove you're a worthy person deserving of admiration and love.

These are things that humans fantasize about—back when most of us were hunters-gatherers and today. I mean, how many of us have estranged, strained, or competitive relationships with siblings? Wish there was something we could have done to have prevented a loved one's death? Dream of proving our worth to those who have doubted us?

I will give you so, so many examples of Universal Fantasies in the coming chapters. And you'll emerge from this reading experience with a thorough understanding of what Universal Fantasy is and how to use it to make everything about the writing and selling of your books better. But for now, think of it this way…

Have you ever watched a Julia Child cooking show? She's going on in her delightful way about whatever she's cooking, and she adds butter. Like, way more butter than you'd imagine that dish—or anyone ever—would need for anything. But, get this, all that butter is why her recipes taste so freaking good.

Universal Fantasy is that **BUTTER**. The ingredient that makes everything from pastries to steak to vegetables way more delicious.

I'll call Universal Fantasy a lot of things in the coming pages: butter, gold, ice cream, lard—even oleo at one point. But mostly, I'll refer to it as butter because it's that special, often uncredited thing that turns nutritious stuff like craft and structure into something readers actually want to consume.

Universal Fantasy is, simply put, **what makes your book taste good**.

CHAPTER FOUR
UNIVERSAL FANTASY VS. TROPE

We'll go into step-by-step instructions about how to identify Universal Fantasies later in the book—I mean, so many. Apologies in advance because by the end of this book, you might be like, "Alright, alright, Theodora. I GET IT!"

But the most important thing to know before we deep dive into Universal Fantasies is…

Universal Fantasy is NOT Trope

Most experienced authors and readers are well-acquainted with tropes, but I'll name a few, just in case:

- road trip buddy adventure
- second-chance romance
- fish-out-of-water
- friends to lovers
- enemies to lovers
- opposites attract

- aliens among us
- time travel
- and my absolute favorite, SECRET BABY. Woo-hoo!

Seriously, the list goes on and on.

But think of the story as a body. And the trope as a brain. The story's trope sets expectations and rules for the kind of story you're going to tell.

If my brain gives my body a command to walk to the kitchen to get another cup of coffee, my body doesn't go outside to do a cartwheel in the sun. No, it gets that sweet, sweet fuel to help me get through the day.

If I market something as a secret baby billionaire romance, there had better be a baby somewhere in the mix—either in the oven or walking around without a clue that their papa is a seriously rich dude who has no idea they exist.

Tropes are built around themes that you and your readers both understand.

Writer: Heyo Reader, this is a Walking for a Cup of Coffee book, not a Doing Cartwheels in the Sun type of book.

Reader 1: Oooh, I lurve Walking for a Cup of Coffee books.

Reader 2: Ugh! I only want to read Cartwheels in the Sun books. Later, skater!

. . .

Most of us can write a decent novel if we have a good story body and a good trope brain.

But have you ever finished a first draft and written *THE END*, only to have it arggh! around like a zombie?

Technically, you wrote a book. And that book did walk to make a cup of coffee. But it kind of lurched there. And the coffee it made, while technically correct, tasted kind of meh and didn't perk you up like it was supposed to.

Let's get real. We've all read and seen zombie stories, right? These are stories that have all the elements of a trope that we love, good craft, and structure but that fail to generate any feeling within us. They're nutritious but not delicious.

Opposites attract. *Okay, well, who cares about either of these people?*

There's a secret baby! This is when you see reader reviews like, *"I don't understand why she didn't tell him. She should have told him. I hate her."*

Friends to Lovers… *Wait, did I just fall asleep waiting for these long-time friends to finally figure out they should be together? What took them so long anyway? That's absurd. They're absurd. Time to bail!*

What's the difference between a zombie book that readers DNF—do not finish— and a BESTSELLER they can't put down?

A beating heart.

Universal Fantasy is what makes that body LIVE. The lifeblood, the muscle, the personality—everything that brings true joy to that first cup of coffee in the morning and doing cartwheels in the sun.

Zombie books feel a little terrible as you're crafting them. Often, you're doing your absolute best while writing one, but you can just feel there's something wrong with it, that it's receiving all the brain signals, but its spirit is gone.

A special note for all my fellow anxious writers who tend to suffer "not good enough" feelings over every book—whether it's destined to be a flop or a bestseller—and especially to newbie writers who genuinely can't tell, here's a simple way I figured out to tell if I had a zombie book on my hands.

When I went to make ads, I couldn't figure out how to sell it, *except with tropes.*

Like, "This is an Opposites Attract romance. You should… uh…totally buy it! It's great. Really. Hey, why aren't you clicking on my ad?"

That's a book on tropes. To be clear, books on tropes can still sell.

If you tell folks you've got a book about a bear and a chicken falling in love, hardcore fans of bear-chicken romances will buy that book.

There's a reason I watch whatever cheesy ensemble romance Netflix puts in front of me *every single holiday season*. I like to watch a diverse array of characters falling in love while Christmas music plays in the background. That's it. When it comes to holiday movies, I don't need anything else, just a diverse ensemble, Christmas music, and lots of falling in love. I'll also watch just about any sci-fi series set on a spaceship (ask me about my enduring love of *Farscape* if you ever meet me IRL) and pretty much anything that involves two teenage boys reluctantly falling in love.

Many readers in my original target audience show up for my books simply because they're IR—precisely the kind of books they want to read. That's awesome. And many writers do and can make a plenty good living on trope books.

But after I discovered the power of Universal Fantasy, I pretty much never had to depend on tropes to write or sell my stories. Blurbs, ads, those awkward party conversations where people ask what you're working on—NO PROBLEM.

With a future bestseller **steeped** in Universal Fantasy, you'll never have any trouble telling people all the appealing details of your book.

Often, for me, it's the opposite.

Now that I've learned to identify the Universal Fantasies in the books I've written, I have to pick a few of the ones featured in the novel to use in ads. And then the fantasies have to *duke it out like Highlander* to figure out which highly clickable ad will sell the most books.

We'll get into how to use Universal Fantasy in ads a little later, but when it comes to tropes versus Universal Fantasy, we'll break Trope vs. UF down this way:

Trope is your story's WHAT IT IS.

Universal Fantasy is your trope's WHY IT'S GOOD.

And when done right, good Universal Fantasy not only gives your trope book LIFE but also **helps it SELL to readers outside your target audience.**

CHAPTER FIVE

BEYOND TROPE: THE MYSTERIOUS CASE OF THE READERS WHO GAVE ME $10K FOR A BOOK WITH A TERRIBLE COVER

Back to that ads class for which I'd paid hundreds of dollars before it dawned on me that I couldn't easily reach my voracious niche audience who always wanted what I was writing, and I would have to learn to sell my books to a much broader audience.

This was a tricky problem, and to solve it, I focused on the first surprise seller of my career, *Her Viking Wolf*.

This was the original cover.

> *What the heck?!*
>
> This book made over 10K in it's first month of sales!
>
> But HOW? And WHY???

Terrible. Just terrible.

Almost all the marketing for this book was either awful or completely nonexistent.

I had no pre-order. No ads. No newsletter swaps—I didn't even have a newsletter back then!

But it did $10,000 in its first month of sales.

W.T.F.?

I used to call *Her Viking Wolf* my white reader book because so many women outside my original target audience found it.

Her Viking Wolf is nine years old at the time of this writing —*ancient* in e-book terms.

But to this day, it converts more readers than most of my contemporaries, and I even used it as the main paranormal reader magnet for the mailing list I finally started a few years later.

For those reasons and more, I decided to use this outlier book to experiment with creating ads that would appeal to readers outside my niche genre.

But to do that, I had to figure out why readers flocked to this book in the first place.

Why was *Her Viking Wolf* a huge convertor of readers outside my original target audience, which was supposed to consist of only modern Black women who were just dying to see another modern Black woman get yanked into the Viking Ages and mated by a huge, red-haired Viking werewolf?

I thought that maybe it was because readers, in general, like Vikings and werewolves and time travel romance.

Perhaps that mashup of genres was enough to get readers outside my original target audience to buy this book.

And for a few readers, that was absolutely correct.

But that couldn't have been the *only* reason why this book became a fan favorite.

After all, other people have written about time-traveling Viking werewolves—yes, it's true, lol!—and they haven't produced the same sales. Some analysis was required to market the book for the first time.

Luckily for me, in this ads class, we were instructed to test our marketing copy and images against each other. One image came out on top of all others. And one piece of copy blew the competition away. To this day (three years later at the time of this writing), this ad still WORKS.

. . .

How? Why?

We'll figure that out in part 3.

But after the success of this ad, I realized that I had been operating on a myth for most of my romance writing career.

I'd assumed that romance readers wanted to read stories featuring only women who looked like them. I'd designed and operated my business on that basic assumption.

But then, how did that explain all of my outside target readers? Or me, for that matter?

Before my thriving six-figure writing career got in the way, I was a voracious romance reader. I was totally addicted to Susan Elizabeth Phillips and J.R. Ward novels—neither of which (at the time) ever featured a character that remotely looked like me. And now I use the few reading hours I have to gobble up male-male romance and Boys Love[1*] EVERYTHING like candy.

But my successful ad campaign proved that I hadn't been giving myself or other romance readers enough credit. While learning how to run profitable Facebook ads, I figured out that when it comes down to bestsellers of ALL genres...

It's not about the characters on the cover...

Or how "good" the book is...

It's all about how well a book or ad taps into a Universal Fantasy.

So meet me in Part 2 to talk about how to mine that Universal Fantasy gold!

---

1. * Boys Love or BL is a manga genre dedicated to romance between two male characters. It's also often referred to as *yaoi*.

PART TWO

MINE THAT UNIVERSAL FANTASY GOLD!

CHAPTER SIX
WHAT CAN UNIVERSAL FANTASY DO FOR YOU?

Shortly after having my epiphany about Universal Fantasy during that 2018 Facebook ads class, I began teaching other writers about UF and how it could be used to write and market better-selling books—even if they were, like mine, in a niche category. The response was outstanding.

I soon began receiving more speaking requests than I could handle while still working as a full-time romance novelist, which is why I decided to write this book. Way better alternative to saying no all the time, right?

And since that first presentation, I've gotten extraordinary feedback from other authors.

Authors who had no idea what to put in marketing copy were suddenly able to figure out how to write powerful, converting ads with UF.

One author gushed that she used UF throughout her book after attending my workshop and was bowled over by the enthusiastic reviews her next release received.

Authors who had been struggling with a story when they came into one of my workshops rushed to thank me afterward because they finally had clarity and could move forward confidently with their story.

Listen, we are all storytellers without a fire.

Me, personally—I have a whole degree in dramatic writing from Carnegie Mellon University. And perhaps figuring that I still just wasn't poor enough, I went on to become a playwright in my later twenties.

I honed my skills with the benefit of rehearsals and later an audience. I could rewrite my plays at every stage of the process until all the lines in my stage work landed. Then I got to sit back and enjoy the show with the audience.

There is nothing—and I mean nothing—on Earth that feels as good as watching an audience enjoy the story you're telling.

So, no. I had never been poorer than during my playwright years, but I missed them after I made the transition to writing novels all by my lonesome.

Unlike our storytelling ancestors who could craft their tales according to the gasps, laughs, and wide-eyed silences of their audiences, many of us writers toil alone with one overarching question hanging over our heads as we type:

Will they like it?

There are so many wonderful craft books out there that tell you how to weave a story and craft character. But as far as I know, there's only one book that addresses the question almost all of us ask ourselves. This one.

. . .

And that's why adding Universal Fantasy to your writing and marketing process has the potential to not only increase your sales but also to allow you to engage with your audience on a storytelling-around-the-fire level.

Would you rather write a good book or a book that builds a forever home inside the heart of your reader?

> **If your answer is the latter, then let's figure out how to identify and use Universal Fantasy to make everything we write DELICIOUS.**

In this part, we'll break down Universal Fantasies with a few case studies of fairy tales—the original bestselling romances.

First up…

CHAPTER SEVEN
PATRON SAINTS OF ROMANCE: DISNEY'S BEAUTY AND THE BEAST

This tale as old as time is so famous, it has its own trope. And there's a reason readers still can't resist a delicious Beauty and the Beast retelling—spoiler alert, *it's CHOCK FULL of UF butter.*

So, let's MINE THIS GOLD!

**TOP TEN
UNIVERSAL FANTASIES
FROM
Disney's
*BEAUTY AND THE BEAST***

***BEAUTY AND THE BEAST* UF 1:**

[Provincial Life] Being forcibly removed from your boring life or somewhere you don't fit in.

I love the Disney version of *Beauty and the Beast* because many of the Universal Fantasies in it also serve as straight-up songs, which makes them even easier to remember and mine for gold.

Take a moment to recall or even watch the "Belle" opening song for either the animated or live-action version of Disney's well-received takes on this fairy tale.

You'll see/remember that Belle is well-read, curious, and thoughtful. And while the French countryside where she lives is beautiful, bustling, and full of fresh-baked bread, alas, she does not fit in or belong in this "provincial life."

She appears doomed to have to make do with her less-than existence until a terrible beast imprisons her father and she offers up herself in exchange for the monster letting her beloved sire go.

With the beast's agreement to her terms, she is instantly ripped out of a life she would never have left on her own.

Yes! Cue the **IRRESISTIBLE** Universal Fantasy.

Listen, as a mom of three, I GET IT. Before I was a mom of three, I got it.

Most women wouldn't officially agree to trade in their dull lives for living in an enchanted castle, but if A BEAST MADE US DO IT… now that's a fantasy!

This particular fantasy was responsible for my one-click of *Keeping Lily*, a bestselling 2017 romance by Izzy Sweet and Sean Moriarty.

I'll set the scene:

There I was in my overly hot kitchen, waiting for a lemon chicken breast and assorted vegetables dish that I knew my children would not eat to finish roasting. My husband would be working late, and I was bored on top of tired after a long, long day of writing and mothering.

Looking for a bit of escape, I casually scanned one of the bestseller lists for a book I'd like to read.

I came across a description with the following scenario:

An outrageously gorgeous mafioso barges into the home of a married man who owes him millions of dollars, ready to kill. Instead of doing whatever it takes to pay off his debt, the horrible husband offers to the mafioso his long-suffering wife, Lily, who is dissatisfied in the marriage and this close to divorcing her feckless, reckless spouse.

But TOO LATE, Lily! The mafioso takes one look at her and accepts her horrible husband's offer.

Thus, the unappreciated wife is ripped from her boring life and marriage and transformed into the treasured obsession of an insanely gorgeous mafioso.

Wait, Lily...

Are you trying to tell me this hot AF mafioso busted up into your house and...

- took you away from your trifling husband
- focused all his attention on YOU, then
- convinced you through the power of mind-blowing sex to accept him as a replacement husband?

Can you imagine me—or any other mom reader—in my kitchen reading this description while feeling under-appreciated? I didn't know this husband-and-wife writing team from Adam back then, but best believe I one-clicked this novel and gulped it down along with a glass of wine after my poorly received dinner.

A few people complain about how much kidnapping and imprisonment there is in romance. This is one of those Universal Fantasies that's not cool (or legal) in real life (IRL). Throughout this book, we'll talk about a lot of fantasies that readers wouldn't necessarily want to happen to them or anyone they know IRL but love to avatar (experience through a fictional character) in entertainment.

However, I'd argue that the perennial attraction to this particular Universal Fantasy isn't about the captivity. It's about being powerfully removed from your boring or ill-fitting present.

Getting forcibly pulled out of your provincial life is a huge fantasy that many women enjoy. It's also a sort of passive heroine call to action that makes many new readers instantly one-click.

BEAUTY AND THE BEAST UF 2:
The bully really likes you

I am so, so happy that negging and gaslighting are now getting the criticism they deserve and that fewer women are falling for mind games and other questionable dating tactics.

Many women aren't interested in anyone who puts them down or is cruel to them in real life.

But in fantasy life?

Gosh, there is just something utterly irresistible about this bully fantasy, which is why it will always sell books.

Bully romance can take many forms. Most are set in the new adult category of high school or college and involve an insanely hot guy—and often his equally hot friends (looking at you, reverse harem). The bully or bullies make the heroine's life miserable until all that tension explodes into hot sex.

And, how thrilling is it when it turns out that your hot bully is secretly obsessed with you?

Cue the primal preen of having the strongest warrior in the village focus all of his attention on you. Also, did you just ferret out a SECRET?! Using my trap music voice to yell out, **"Dopamine! Dopamine! Dopamine!"**

Bully romances are basically the literary equivalent of a hate fuck and perhaps speak to something deep inside of us that desires approval—and in an interesting dichotomy, to somehow quell and stand up to the people who hurt us.

In romance, ALL attention is good attention. And for many readers, that focused attention feels even better when it comes from someone who is mean to you because they secretly like you.

Bonus UF Butter: Reverse-Bully fantasies also melt well over bestselling hotcakes. The guy who's an asshole to everyone else but becomes a big ol' teddy bear for you? Ooohhh...TAKE MY MONEY!

BEAUTY AND THE BEAST UF 3:

Abuse of Power

The Beast uses aggression and power to take away all of Belle's choices.

In real life, "ugh!" but in fantasy life, "okay, now!"

"Bossholes" remain perennial favorites even among readers who would head straight to HR if a real-life superior pulled any of this stuff.

Remember, readers are often entertained by and love to fantasize about things they wouldn't necessarily want to happen to them in real life.

As someone who grew up ultrareligious, I have to say **it is so much fun to read and see NAUGHTY and WRONG things.**

Some of the best Universal Fantasies go against a reader's real-life morals. And you should keep an eye out for these opposite-of-real-life fantasies because they are GOLD.

BEAUTY AND THE BEAST UF 4:

SIXTEEN CANDLES (the most popular guy/richest guy in school CHOOSES you!)

Even though it's pretty vague as to exactly what kind of prince The Beast is or what faraway land—within a short horse-and-buggy ride of provincial France—he rules over (without anyone knowing he's there), the fact remains that he's technically the wealthiest and most high-status guy Belle has ever encountered. So when he **chooses her** to break the curse—BUTTER!

Sixteen Candles was, hands down, my favorite romantic movie back in the day, but it is so problematic now. Between the racist depictions and lack of consent, I won't even allow my kids to watch it.

However, there is one thing this movie got perennially right.

Being seen as special by the richest, hottest, most popular guy in school—that doesn't just feel good, that feels *delicious*.

Perhaps this hearkens back to a time when being chosen by the right man was the equivalent of winning the lottery.

Not only do you get the primal preen of attracting the desirable guy all the other girls are talking about, but you also get that beauty pageant-winner feeling.

This UF works particularly well for pre-meets. This is simply the paragraphs or pages that introduce the hero to the main character before they formally meet.

Think of the billionaire boss whose reputation and credentials precede him into the main character's life. He's the equivalent of a god she's only heard about until they meet in a huge, exciting way when he comes down from Mt. Olympus.

Or recall *Twilight*, in which we stare along with Bella at the mesmerizing guy in the cafeteria. We're told by our new friend that this gorgeous creature never dates *anyone*. Yet, a few chapters and huge reveals later, we're making our parking lot debut as a high school couple with *the* Edward Cullen. BUTTER!

One of the best changes that the 2005 movie adaptation of *Pride and Prejudice* makes from its source material is adding a high-status guy pre-meet.

The frolicking dancers come to a dead stop when Mr. Darcy appears in the ballroom flanked by three supporting characters. And the host of the ball rushes forward to thank him for coming. As he strides forward, our heroine, Elizabeth Bennet, is told that he earns TWICE as much as the eligible bachelor the Bennet girls have come to the ball to meet. And then…

OMG! OMG! OMG! The stiff and superior gentleman-god VISIBLY reacts when he sets eyes on Lizzy. Chest clasp!

That's why books centered around this fantasy have been bestsellers since the creation of bestseller charts.

. . .

BEAUTY AND THE BEAST UF 5:

[BE OUR GUEST] Servants who are delighted to serve!

Aw, who doesn't remember "Be Our Guest" from the Disney version of *Beauty and the Beast?*

It centers around one of the fantasies we don't often talk about out loud.

SERVANTS who are *delighted* to serve

Back to me being a mom of three who only cooks because she has to.

Would I love it if my appliances and dishes came to life to do the job for me? You bet!

I mean, who wouldn't want to have someone completely trustworthy swoop in to do it all happily, leaving you without any guilt whatsoever?

J.R. Ward's *doggens*—a servant race within her paranormal world that just LIVES to serve her main characters—are a great example of this fantasy done well.

And who doesn't love a contemporary billionaire hero who comes with a complete staff, falling all over themselves to make you comfortable, make you over (more on that UF later), and make you love the hero even more because they happily take on pesky real-life duties like cleaning, cooking, childcare, and driving[1*]?

***BEAUTY AND THE BEAST* UF 6:**
A Fixer-Upper

My husband was what I like to call turn-key when we met. He was six years divorced, so he'd gone through ALL the marriage counseling but enough years ago that he was healed and ready to love again.

He knew how to listen. He was great at communication. He could fix seemingly anything. He had an impressive job, and he thought I was wonderful even though I was a starving playwright prone to fits of anxiety and depression.

He was awesome, so his profession of love three months into our relationship completely baffled me.

"But why do you love me?" I asked him. "I don't get it. You've got your act together. You're a great guy with a great career. Why would you want to be with someone like me?"

He assured me I was also great. And he reminded me that he was seven years older than me.

"I don't think you'll be a starving playwright seven years from now. You've got so much potential."

So yeah, he was perfect for me, and I was super happy to marry this wonderful guy almost exactly two years after our first date.

But this weird thing happened when we got pregnant the first time and went to look for a new house. We searched and searched, but he didn't love any of the places we looked at, which I found a bit odd.

But okay, instead of buying a house, we ended up renting...for THREE YEARS. That's three years of looking at house after house that I liked just fine but that my husband didn't spark with for one reason or another.

However, he turned out to be right about my potential.

Over those three years, I finally got a handle on my anxiety, launched Theodora Taylor, and earned enough extra income for daycare, Hawaii vacations, *and* a down payment on a house. I also got pregnant again—this time with twins.

So much good fortune, but we'd reached a crisis point. We needed a bigger place that would fit our expanding family. But my husband still couldn't commit to a house. I was sure we'd have to rent again, which was…let's just say, *frustrating* when you're several months pregnant with twins.

But then my husband found this weird short sell in Burbank, a great LA neighborhood with a stellar school district, and he asked our saint of a realtor to arrange yet another tour.

At five months pregnant, we toured it, and ugly wasn't even the word to describe it. The guy who owned the house was a hunter who had gone through a bitter divorce. The place was a mess. There was clutter EVERYWHERE.

From the musky smell of it, the owner used the fireplace to cook meat, and the walls were dingy with what I could only hope was soot. Deer heads hung on every wall, staring at us morosely as we took the tour.

My husband decided to be kind, I thought, and he had a long talk with the owner about how much he liked the house, their mutual affection for old cars, and how they were in similar professional unions.

Then we left—and as soon as we stepped out onto the sidewalk, my husband asked our realtor to put in a competitive offer for this place.

Without even consulting me!

I was like, "What the heck, dude?!"

"This is a short sell at an amazing price in Burbank," he answered.

"Yeah, but the house is ugly!" I pointed out.

When I said that, my husband looked even more confused. "What? That house is *amazing*! It's the right size, and it's got great bones. Don't you see its potential?"

That's when I realized my husband hadn't been looking for the perfect house like I had been. He'd been looking for the perfect fixer-upper all along. And when he found it, it was love at first sight.

And then I thought about how much he'd helped me transform and overcome my personal demons over the years, and another realization hit me like a Mack truck. "Oh, my God, I'm the Fixer Upper! That's why he fell in love with me!"

So the point of that long backstory is that the fixer-upper fantasy works both in real life and the fantasy worlds we create.

It drives relationships.

AND it keeps HGTV on cable channels around the world because pretty much the entire globe agrees *Fixer-uppers are IRRESISTIBLE.*

This is why billionaire alphaholes who are fixed by the love of an incredible woman will stay earning money *until the end of time*.

Just like people will stay till the end of an episode of *Fixer Upper* to see the big reveal, readers will keep swiping to see that final transformation of an alphahole hero to someone worthy of the heroine's love.

Here are few more super-quick examples of powerful UFs featured in Disney's *Beauty and the Beast*.

BEAUTY AND THE BEAST UF 7:

Wounded Main Character in need of love, healing, and understanding

Oh man, I LOVE a good wound. Characters who have been damaged emotionally and/or physically are some of my absolute favorites in ALL GENRES. Jack Ryan, Wolverine, practically every single character in a Sarah J. Maas novel…I adore them all. And guess what? Readers love them too.

Humans, quiet as it's kept, are deeply social animals who want to help each other. The Beast has been turned into a literal beast—at this point, he's suffered as a monster for longer than he was ever human. This is a wound that can only be healed by love.

The same goes for Christian Grey, the star of EL James's mega-bestselling Fifty Shades series. He's been emotionally and psychologically damaged by things that happened in his past.

Real life: Dude, engage a therapist.

Fantasy life: Hello, Anastasia!

If you want to give your reader the same feeling they get when they nurse a wounded bird back to flight, make sure your hero has a wound that can only be healed by the love and attention of their perfect partner.

BEAUTY AND THE BEAST UF 8:

Not just any gift. The RIGHT GIFT.

This is another fantasy that works well in both the real and fantasy worlds.

When someone gives you something you wouldn't have thought or dared to want, that person earns a special place in your heart.

How many of us don't remember Beast giving Belle that library?

I'm still sighing!

Why? Because a library full of more books than anyone could possibly read in one lifetime is the *exact right gift* for a character who adores reading. This present tells Belle and the viewer that the Beast doesn't think she's just beautiful like Gaston does. He truly *sees her*.

BEAUTY AND THE BEAST UF 9:

I'M STILL TEAM JACOB (the love triangle)

Both Gaston and The Beast want Belle. YES! Love triangles!

Real Talk: The only thing tastier than being chosen by a romance hero is having two of them fight over you. They can be from rival paranormal crews (vampires vs. werewolves in *Twilight*), two different times in your life (past vs. present in *The Hunger Games*), two different sides of the tracks (rich Cal vs. poor Jack in *Titanic*), two brothers (why did I watch all eight seasons of *Vampire Diaries*?)—seriously, the buttery scenarios are unending.

And sometimes, the rivals even figure out how to SHARE. I see you, fanfic for all of the above, menage, and all that delicious reverse harem.

BEAUTY AND THE BEAST UF 10:

[*SHE'S ALL THAT*] A really, really good MAKEOVER!

As someone who changed out her hair every other month before the pandemic, let me tell you there is nothing better than a really good makeover.

Every reader dreamed at one point of who they could be with better hair, the right clothes, and a you-can-do-it '80s montage sequence.

And keep in mind that a good makeover isn't just limited to the external stuff.

My Fair Lady ain't a classic for nothing. Opinions on the domineering Henry Higgins come and go. Still, audiences never tire of watching Eliza Doolittle transform from a Cockney-spewing street-peddler into a fine lady who can successfully masquerade as a duchess at an embassy ball.

However, my favorite Makeover of all time is *The Karate Kid* —both the '80s and the post-millennium kung fu versions! There's just something about watching this kid go from knowing absolutely nothing about martial arts to winning a major competition that stirs the "You Can Do It" spirit in all of us.

I also love MCs who…

- start businesses
- win huge competitions after lots of hard work and personal epiphanies
- pull off major character arcs like learning to stand up for themselves

Transforming into someone you didn't know you were capable of being is one of the most enduring human fantasies.

In the now super-obscure documentary, *20 Dates*, the great screenwriting teacher, Robert McKee, said that a good romance isn't about two people falling in love, but two people becoming who they need to be to *deserve love*.

The Beast transforms from an illiterate spoiled monster into a humble gentleman, capable of reading, conversing, and eating neatly with his captive. He not only gives her gifts that matter—like the library and a glimpse of her beloved sire in his magic mirror—he also puts Belle's needs before his own by letting her go when she sees that her father needs her. Talk about a total makeover into someone deserving of love!

. . .

Belle also gets a makeover. She goes from struggling as an unappreciated, dismissed, and objectified villager to the *belle of the ball*. Watching her waltz with a prince several levels above her supposed station who values both her beauty and her intelligence is a massive part of what makes the Disney version of this romance so special.

This Universal Fantasy hits viewers hard because don't we all crave (and hopefully have someone) who transforms us into the best version of ourselves through the power of their love and attention?

I know this fixer-upper did!

BONUS *BEAUTY AND THE BEAST* UF:
Banging a Beast

Sleeping with a beast is one of those secret fantasies that doesn't get talked about often enough.

But there's a reason that Beast, not the human he transformed back into at the end of the movie, is part of the Disney parade. A lot of women secretly want to bang a beast.

Remember that.

Especially if you're writing alien romance.

So you can see why Beauty and the Beast remains one of the most enduring fairy tales of all time—it's filled with SO MUCH Universal Fantasy butter. Like, way more butter than you'd ever think anyone would need for one movie dish.

And this brings us to our first piece of homework...

HOMEWORK

Remember your comfort food movie--not your favorite movie—your *comfort food* movie. I'm talking about the movie you watch with a tub of ice cream when you've had a bad day.

I no longer rewatch movies due to the ability to enjoy doing so having been broken by the raising of three children. But back before that happened, my go-to comfort food movie was *Jerry Maguire*.

So recall this movie you love so much, and see if you can identify any of the *Beauty and the Beast* Top 10 Universal Fantasies in it. There's usually at least one.

For extra points, make a list of at least three new Universal Fantasies you can spot and write a short sentence about why it's a UF.

Remember, a Universal Fantasy isn't just the what. It's the WHY.

With apologies to *Jerry Maguire*, which I unfortunately no longer remember well enough to break down, I'll use *The Color Purple*, my official favorite movie of all time, as an example. I centered my college thesis around the novel, which Alice Walker published in 1982. And despite my broken rewatch ability, I've seen the stage play FOUR times.

***Beauty and the Beast* UF:** *Makeover.* The "ugly" heroine Celie gets a makeover and is transformed into someone who can stand up to her abusive husband by the love and attention of Shug Avery.

New UF 1: *Siblings reunited.* Almost all siblings eventually split up and go on to live their separate lives. So this reunion transcends race and time period to resonate with sisters from all walks of life and ethnicities. Before I went off to college, this ending slightly moved me. Afterward, it made me ugly cry. And it doesn't matter how many fights brothers Randall and Kevin get into on *This is Us*. I'm a mess every time they make up.

New UF2: *Being serenaded by someone who can really sing.* This UF was also featured in "Open Mic," my absolute favorite episode of *Schitt's Creek*. Nothing makes you feel more special than having all of someone's attention in song! It's *simply the best*. And man, can you understand Celie falling hard for Shug after she stops her raucous show to lay the utterly soul-piercing "Sister" on her?

New UF3: *Parent's forgiveness.* Yet another fantasy that works in both real and fantasy life. It is physically impossible to keep your eyes dry while watching that sinful Shug being accepted back into her estranged preacher father's loving arms.

---

1. * I cannot overemphasize driving enough. I hate driving in real life, and few of my heroines do it if they don't have to. Writer fantasy unlocked!

CHAPTER EIGHT
PATRON SAINTS OF ROMANCE: DISNEY'S CINDERELLA

**Top 5 Universal Fantasies
From
Disney's *CINDERELLA***

CINDERELLA **UF 1:**

Instalove

Say what you want about instalove, but readers adore it.

Love at first sight, fated mates—these Universal Fantasies endure because relationships are HARD in real life.

In an uncertain world with a 50/50 chance of divorce, it's nice to imagine a love that is blessed by fate and meant to be.

And as much as people make fun of Disney princess movies where the prince falls, at first sight, I think Cinderella has one of the best versions of that theme.

The prince is tired and exasperated by the same ole, same ole. He's Victorian-era swiping left on all the eligible bachelorettes in the land. Ain't none of these women getting a rose. But then...

He sees a fair maiden prettier and shinier than all the rest. Yo! Girl even has her own spotlight!

Of course, he's going to fall in love with her immediately.

He's never seen or experienced anything like the made over Cinderella.

And you can easily see why they're a true match.

CINDERELLA UF 2:

True Love Match

Meeting your one true match is a fantastic Universal Fantasy.

And Kennedy Ryan's RWA-Award winning *Long Shot* provides a superb modern example of how this particular UF can compel readers like no other.

We meet the book's main character, a basketball player, the night before a big game.

He walks into a bar and sees...

HER.

This beautiful, vivacious woman, yelling at a basketball game on the screen.

They get to talking and wow, wow, *WOW!* She's smart and knows her basketball; she's funny and gorgeous. She's also a great listener.

They're both biracial, and they end up in this deep conversation that lets us readers know these two BELONG TOGETHER.

But then they walk out of the bar, and when he tries to take their meet-perfect further, she says, "I already have a boyfriend."

NOOOOOOOO!!!!

I repeat, NOOOOOOOOOOOOOOOOOOOOO!!!!!!!!

I started reading this book on Black Friday morning in 2018, and I could not stop swiping.

I didn't shop for deals. I didn't eat breakfast. Eventually, my kids demanded food.

With my Kindle app open on my phone, I warmed up some Thanksgiving leftovers on one plate and threw it down on the coffee table, commanding them to eat—like dogs—before returning to my room with my precious novel.

This book turned me into a terrible mother because I just couldn't stop reading until these two people who were so obviously meant to be together found their way to a happy ending.

This is another fantasy that touches something primal and social inside of us. Let's not forget that until modern times, marriages in many societies on all six inhabited continents were mostly arranged.

As a contemporary parent of three, of course, I want my kids to pick their own spouses—but do I? I mean, do I really? Like, will I have some opinions that will slip out if my goofy oldest twin brings home someone who doesn't fully complement and appreciate her oddball nature?

Let's just say I'm practicing holding my tongue, but the chances of me staying non-invasive in that scenario are about the same as the current divorce rate.

Whatever the present-day trend, that matchmaking instinct lurks inside many of us.

That's why True Love Match is a super compelling Universal Fantasy that keeps readers swiping even when they should be mothering, working, and sleeping.

CINDERELLA UF 3:

Suffering Main Character

Another great Universal Fantasy that *Cinderella* does well is the suffering main character.

I adore a down-and-out main character.

So many people I encounter in real life are suffering in some way, and there's nothing I can do about it. As of this writing, my husband has had to cancel our *New York Times* subscription for a fourth time because I was getting so upset about things I couldn't control happening to other people around the world.

But with romance novels, you know that if the main character is suffering at the beginning of the story, their love interest will help end her suffering by the end of it.

One of the best examples of this is *Lover Eternal* by J.R. Ward.

The novel starts with a good-hearted plain-Jane heroine receiving news that her aggressive cancer is back and that it's terminal this time.

She accepts that she's going to die.

But WAIT!

A Hollywood-level hot hero with a raging beast inside him comes along, and his love heals her in so many ways.

Lover Eternal is a glorious, deeply satisfying read because it taps into the Universal Fantasy of ending the suffering of someone good WITH LOVE.

My favorite Boys Love manga series of all time is *Ten Count* by Rihito Takarai.

In this series, our main character, Tadaomi Shirotani, lives with an obsessive-compulsive disorder that manifests as severe germaphobia.

This disorder has not only crippled him emotionally and socially but also physically hurt him. He washes his hands so much, they've become chapped and raw to the point that they bleed through the white gloves he always wears in public.

These spots of blood draw the attention of Riku Kurose, a ridiculously hot therapist who offers to help him. And oh my gosh, the reader feels so much relief when Shirotani accepts his offer.

Our suffering hero will finally get the help he needs.

But just as Kurose's methods are beginning to work for Shirotani, the therapist abruptly ends their sessions—why? [Trap voice: Secret! Secret! Secret! **Dopamine! Dopamine! Dopamine!**]

Shirotani has to track him down to find out the answer... which is that Kurose has fallen in love with him!!! And thus, it would be inappropriate for him to continue as Shirotani's therapist...

Real Life: Yes, that is exactly right, good sir. Cease and desist this relationship immediately. Story over. Nothing more to see here, folks.

Fantasy Life: NOOOOOOOOO, Kurose!!! Not only are you two a True Love Match that MUST be together, but we also know Shirotani's suffering won't be alleviated until he receives some seriously unorthodox reversion therapy, outrageously hot sex, and TRUE LOVE.

Luckily for me, the author/illustrator went with the Fantasy Life version, and I couldn't download and read all six volumes of this series fast enough. I just had to make it to the end of Shirotani's suffering.

This is the same reason why we love the ending of *Cinderella*.

Not only does she win the prince, but also, her suffering is now over.

Speaking of the Prince...

CINDERELLA UF 4:

Obsessed Prince

I love this dude. When Cinderella runs off, he doesn't just say, "Crap, guess that didn't work out."

He gives his royal guard *the single shoe she left behind* and DEMANDS that they hunt down the girl who got away.

This is an excellent example of the obsessed hero.

And obsessed heroes **SELL BOOKS!**

Note that the elements of bestselling stories that critics most often sneer at—think about all the derisive copy Edward Cullen's habit of watching Bella while she sleeps inspired—are often the butter that makes books taste so good.

In real life, "stop calling me" means "stop calling me." Seriously, dude. Stop!

But in fantasy life, readers love a man who will stop at nothing to get his woman.

Again, ATTENTION = BUTTER in fantasy life.

So the idea of a delicious hero watching over you, even when you sleep—and/or refusing to let you go, even when you run—taps into several security fantasies for readers.

We'll talk more later about how entertainment provides a safe, almost virtual place for us humans to explore and experience their fantasies. But for now, suffice it to say that the obsessed hero just plain works in romance novels.

And in this case, the prince's obsession SAVES Cinderella from a life of misery under her stepmother's thumb.

Actually, that big save brings us to one of the most misunderstood Universal Fantasies in *Cinderella*...

CINDERELLA UF 5:

Badass Cinderella

Quite a few people classify this fairy tale ending as a simple case of a woman being saved by a man.

But I'd argue that Cinderella is a badass *who saved herself*.

Cinderella has zero resources and has been relegated to the role of live-in servant.

But she manages to raise a mouse and bird army.

This small creature militia…

- helps her with her work
- watches out for her at all times
- makes her an original dress for the ball
- is totally okay with shapeshifting to get her to that ball
- lets her out of her locked room when the prince's guard came through

I mean, they, like, always have her back.

Dude, I can't get my three kids to clean their rooms on a consistent basis! This is no small feat. She's an original #GirlBoss.

Some people assume that women have this fantasy of being saved by a prince. But I think most women dream of getting the opportunity to *save themselves*.

That's why the Disney *Cinderella* ending works so much better than the 17th century Charles Perrault fairytale ending of her simply trying on the shoe and having it fit…

Please take a moment to (re-)watch the ending of Disney's *Cinderella*. Trust, if you haven't had to watch it countless times like me, you probably don't remember how badass that ending was....

BONUS *CINDERELLA* UF:

Pluck Rewarded

AAAAnd cue the huge wedding scene after Cinderella and her mouse army throttle that happy ending into the station.

This Universal Fantasy works because Cinderella earns her prince and wedding through perseverance and pluck. #PrincessPersisted

On a hard sci-fi note, I'd argue that the titular character of *The Martian* by Andy Weir is a persistent Cinderella. All the things the main character must do and overcome to "get saved" is the highly buttered steak of that book and its equally satisfying movie version. #AstronautPersisted

HOMEWORK

Find and read a short romance centered around a Beauty and the Beast or Cinderella Universal Fantasy. If you want a suggestion, Jessa Kane's *Making Their Vows* and *Breaking the Bully* both pack an extremely naughty UF punch.

If you prefer audio, check out the Read Me Romance podcast. So many of my favorite romance authors have written stories for this awesome program, and many of them contain Cinderella UFs.

OR

Grab a beloved novel and find your favorite part.

Highlight and/or note any and everything that strikes you as a UF.

Pay special attention to sections, actions, and pieces of dialogue that elicit a bodily reaction—tummy flutters, heart palpitations, lost breaths, stirrings below the waist… anything that literally gives you the feels—and figure out the universal **WHY**.

CHAPTER NINE
MODERN SAINTS OF ROMANCE: SHONDA SHOWS

> I scream, you scream,
> we all scream for
> Shonda Rhimes ice cream—
> because it's chock full of
> Universal Fantasy butter.

I consider myself a pretty disciplined writer. When I have a book due, I arise around four in the morning, make myself a cup of coffee, pull a daily tarot card, meditate for a bit, and get to work by 5 a.m.

I clock words before yoga, then more words before lunch, and then more words before my kids get home. I don't turn on the TV until a prescribed time after dinner when it's time to curl up on the couch with my husband. If there's a show I want to watch by myself, I save it for a nice binge between books. I see you, *Gossip Girl* reboot—at least I will when I'm done writing this Universal Fantasy book.

I am, dear fellow scribe, a paragon of writerly discipline.

Except on Fridays.

What makes Fridays different, you might wonder.

Well, there is one show…one show that never fails to kryptonite my Friday writing routine when it is delivering new episodes. We'll call it THE SHOW.

And whenever I make a project writing schedule while THE SHOW is putting out new episodes, my long-suffering voice of reason pipes up for yet another conversation about my magical thinking.

Voice of Reason: Mayhap, madame, you should make Fridays a half-day—or at the very least, block out an hour after lunch to watch THE SHOW. You'll recall what happened every Friday during the last book.

Me: No, not *every* Friday. There was that one Friday when I stuck to the schedule LIKE A BOSS.

Voice of Reason: Do you mean the Friday when THE SHOW failed to post a new episode to Hulu?

Long silence.

Me: It will be different this time. This time, I'll be able to resist THE SHOW. It will not draw me away from my own work with its scrumptious cases and delicious workplace romance crumbs. And I won't continue to chase those feelings by stacking an episode of *This is Us* on top of it, along with all those *9-1-1*s that are somehow never not piled up and waiting for me on Hulu.

Voice of Reason: Madame, might I suggest—

Me: IT WILL BE DIFFERENT THIS TIME.

Narrator [with a sad trombone]: *It was not different this time. Alas, Theodora lost loads of crucial writing hours to THE SHOW and its cohorts.*

So, three things:

1. You're wondering what show this is. You know what show this is because you've gotten all the context clues from the section header and my protests, and it's pretty obvious. But you are still braced for the thrill of me confirming that it is *Grey's Anatomy* because YOU WERE RIGHT!

Trap voice: **Dopamine! Dopamine! Dopamine!**

Readers love to be surprised. They also love to be right. Remember that bonus UF.

2. Dude, I have no idea why my Voice of Reason talks with a high-falutin' British accent. What does yours sound like?

3. It almost doesn't matter what episodic show I was talking about. I'm pretty sure most people have a show like this—one they cannot resist the same way my lactose-intolerant butt can't stay out of a Ben & Jerry's on a super-hot day.

But Shonda Rhimes, or Shonda, as I call her—because she's my imaginary bestie, and I may or may not have WWSD? (what would Shonda do?) Post-Its on my wall—excels at making the kind of rich story ice cream viewers cannot resist.

So let's mine a few of her greatest executive producer hits for some of that Universal Fantasy gold. But this time, you'll help me with the list.

If you haven't seen the show I'm talking about, no worries. Simply replace it with an episode you love with a similar setup. I'll even make comp show suggestions under each category.

Just be aware that most of my UF references will be from early seasons of each show, when they were at the height of their popularity and most addictive.

GREY'S ANATOMY: PILOT STUDY

Comp Shows: *Anything that revolves around cases (ex. 9-1-1, CSI, NCIS, etc.)*

I love that *Grey's* started out as a mid-season replacement. Maybe the television execs couldn't tell they had a bottomless bowl of ice cream in their hands when they slotted GA into the 2004–05 schedule as a backup show, but audiences ate it up from the start.

Let's figure out what made the *Grey's Anatomy* pilot so yummy and irresistible.

Grey's **UF 1:**

That one night stand is THE ONE (and also your new boss)

In the opening scene of *Grey's Anatomy*, Meredith rushes away from a one-night stand with some hunk whose name she can't remember. It's her first day on the job, and she doesn't want to be late, she explains before telling him not to be there when she gets done with her shower.

Meredith is a surgical intern with ambition and something to prove. She has no time or emotional patience for a one-night stand who wants to chat the next morning.

So how shocked is she when that one-night stand turns out to be Dr. Derek Shepherd, her attending neurosurgeon—the medical equivalent of her boss???!!!

Surprise! Twist! Chance for us to squirm through the awkward re-meet with Meredith without actually—you know—having to ever deal with this situation ourselves in real life. Though, I'd argue that if this ever did happen to any of us romance readers, we'd know exactly what to do because we've seen the scenario play out so often.

This is one of those vanilla ice cream fantasies that has been done in every sort of iteration since. I've seen the same thing happen with billionaire CEO bosses, stepbrother bosses, werewolf bosses—I'm fairly sure it had to have happened on a sci-fi TV show or movie at least once, but I just can't recall it (totally let me know if your remember one, though).

Some readers complain vociferously about this UF. "It's so overdone. We've seen this before!" they whine.

Yeah, yeah, yeah. We've all eaten vanilla ice cream before.

Again, I'm lactose intolerant, and I'm supposed to be on keto right now—but if Dr. Derek Shepherd offered me a vanilla ice cream cone? Forget keto! I'm eating that vanilla ice cream cone. I'm scarfing it down. Because it's yummy and familiar, and I know **I'LL ENJOY IT**.

Don't dismiss vanilla ice cream fantasies. Readers love them. They're crazy dependable and super sellable.

. . .

Grey's UF 2:

Racers, start your engines… [Competition Avatar Butter]

Two minutes into the pilot episode of *Grey's Anatomy* the chief of staff, Dr. Richard Webber gives a speech in which he instructs the new crop of surgical interns to say hello to their competition. He lets them know that eight of the people they greet will switch to an easier specialty. Five will crack under the pressure. And two will be asked to leave. He tells them that this hospital is their starting line—their arena.

Ah, competition. Every four years (give or take, depending on the pandemic), I hunt down a live television feed somewhere and post up in front of the television screen to watch the Summer Olympics.

I tell you, this is the human avatar experience at its best. We might wind easily after two minutes of cardio, but during the Games, we can almost feel our avatar's muscles working as we flip, spin, spike, jump hurdles, and stick all sorts of landings.

So how invested are we in these *Grey's* characters who are told within the first TWO minutes of the show that they are in the fight of their life? People who love to compete, people who hate to compete—it doesn't matter which team we are on, we all fall hard for the competition in this show.

Hunger Games by Suzanne Collins, quidditch matches in *Harry Potter*, and *Total Drama*, that insanely irritating *Survivor/Amazing Race* cartoon rip-off my kids won't stop watching—they all let us experience competition. You know, without us having to actually compete.

Through character avatars, we get to experience the rushes, thrills, and validation of victory without having to risk anything in our real lives. How cool is that? *I've had a hard day, darling. Let's pull off a ground-breaking surgery and kip off to bed, shall we?*

Bonus Competition Fantasy: Overcoming your parental privilege

Meredith is the daughter of an extraordinary glass ceiling-shattering doctor, Ellis Grey. The first decade or so of the show involves Meredith proving to herself and everyone else that she is just as good a doctor as her mother, if not better. And yay, she does, so take THAT all you people who said she breezed into med school because her mother was Ellis Grey!

I'll admit, as the African American daughter of non-writer parents, I don't particularly get why we Americans love the fantasy of overcoming parental privilege. But hey, who am I to judge? I love it too. Like, a prince who has to take over his father's throne in a questionable non-democratic monarchy—I'll read that all day.

Actually, while writing this, a friend recommended *American Royals* by Katharine McGee, an alternative-timeline young adult novel in which the author reimagines the lives of the descendants of George Washington—the first king of America. *What?! One-click!*

Main point: This UF is another perennial favorite.

Grey's **UF 3:**

Comeback kids [Dropping Your Character's Ice Cream to Set Them Up for a UF]

Meredith Grey drops her ice cream big-time in the pilot.

Ice Cream Drop! She's derided by the intern group's most vicious competitor, Cristina Yang, as a product of nepotism.

Comeback! She gets in prickly Cristina's good graces by offering her the scrub-in spot for a surgery they win by accurately figuring out the reason for a patient's mysterious seizures.

Ice Cream Drop! But then she falls right back out of Cristina's graces again when her smoking hot new boss says she's the one who will scrub in for the surgery—no matter what she promised Cristina.

Comeback! All seems lost, but then Meredith proves she's one to watch by doing well during the surgery. She wins the respect of both the hot attending and her vicious fellow surgical intern, who, in later episodes, will go on to become "her person"—her lifelong best friend.

This is just a microcosm of the comeback butter Shonda Rhimes and her writing table insert into so many ice cream plots throughout the series—bringing their characters to the lowest point, then giving them a comeback we can all cheer for.

Think of it this way. In a volleyball game, you don't just spike out of nowhere. The ball must drop in order to be set up for one of those magnificent moves.

I adore how this show uses the flip side of a fantasy to set up the spike of a good comeback. It constantly tears down its characters so that the audience can experience the agony of defeat *and then* the joy of a comeback. Sometimes within the same episode, but sometimes over the course of seasons.

I mean, who can forget Izzy, another surgical intern, who was introduced in the pilot as a bubbly former model who should perhaps not be taken seriously? She ends up transforming into an amazing and charitable doctor—after the love of her life dies terribly and abruptly.

What if your worst fear came true and you rise like a phoenix from the ashes of your low point?

With a good comeback fantasy, your audience can feel that joy without any of the pesky real-life turmoil.

Now it's your turn. Watch the *Grey's Anatomy* pilot—or any pilot for one of your ice cream series, and mine at least three Universal Fantasies. Don't forget to include the WHY.

SCANDAL: CHARACTER STUDY

Comp Shows: *Any sci-fi series or sitcom with a colorful cast. (ex.* Battlestar Galactica, Firefly, Modern Family, Brooklyn 9-9, *etc.)*

In part 3, we'll talk more about infusing your characters with Universal Fantasy, but for now, let's break down what made some of the characters in this show so yummy.

SCANDAL CHARACTER UF 1:

Diego "Huck" Muñoz, Faithful Dog

Aw, who can forget Huck, the tortured former black-ops agent/assassin-turned-utterly-devoted-handler/killer/whatever-Olivia-wanted-him-to-doer?

Dogs were the first animals domesticated by humans, and there's a special primal place in our hearts for any animal (human or otherwise) who protects us, loves us unconditionally, and attacks on command.

For other examples of this faithful dog UF, see Boyle from *Brooklyn 9-9* and Amos Burton, my absolute favorite character on *The Expanse*. Amos is a mechanic and extremely devoted to the ship's engineer, Naomi Nagata. He'll growl if you so much as look at her the wrong way, and don't tell her boyfriend, but I'm still shipping these dedicated friends.

Series characters imbued with this UF butter make for terrific side characters and even better heroes when they focus all that no-questions-asked loyalty and devotion on a deserving love.

SCANDAL **CHARACTER UF 2**
Olivia Pope, Slay-All-Day WonderGoddess

Kerry Washington is a fantastic actress. She deserves all the awards and all the kudos she's gotten for her incredible on-screen work. She also happens to be—at least in this role—a perfect example of what many American women fantasize about...

Her Thinness requires no lifestyle changes or dieting—just an occasional swim when she's upset and needs to think.

Her Immaculately Tailored Clothes require no shopping. I get overwhelmed at Nordstrom Rack and pretty much live in muumuus and sweats. Olivia Pope has a killer endless wardrobe just magically hanging in her closet.

Her Hair and Skin require no maintenance. *You* may struggle with adult acne and finding time to visit the salon. But Olivia Pope came out of the womb with flawless skin and a perfectly laid blowout.

We might ask why Olivia treats the men in her life the way she does. But we never ask why they're so obsessed with her. I mean, look at her—actually, that's precisely what so many of us used to tune in live to do every Thursday while tweeting things like "that coat!" and "how is she so pretty???"

This makes her a fantastic avatar as she navigates her way through political intrigue, "handles" shocking twists, and stands over a ton of dead bodies in stiletto heels and her iconic elbow-length leather gloves.

If you love or have a talent for fashion and/or makeup, don't be afraid to channel your inner costume designer and add that butter to your MC's look. The titular character in

Sophie Kinsella's *Shopaholic* gave me so much of this kind of ice cream that I honestly couldn't blame her for going into debt to support her habit.

For other examples of the Slay-All-Day WonderGoddess, see Carrie from *Sex in the City*, Beyoncé in any of her video albums, and Elektra in *Pose*.

SCANDAL CHARACTER UF 3

President Fitzgerald "Fitz" Grant. The most powerful man in the free world (or your story world) is obsessed with YOU

What's the only thing better than an obsessed prince? An obsessed KING, baby!

If UF is butter, then POWER is *truffle butter*.

For first in series especially, don't be afraid to slather your main character's love interest in power. Kings, alien emperors, CEOs, shifter pack alphas, mafia crimelords—readers will forever enjoy watching these hugely powerful characters get taken down…by love.

Bonus Character UF:

We are Family! [Created Families]

If you ever have a chance to attend a talk by Dr. Jennifer Lynn Barnes about the psychology of fandom, please do yourself the favor of going. One of the many valuable things she covers is how the foundations of some of our most beloved entertainments are Created Families.

. . .

As of this writing, Dr. Miranda Bailey and Dr. Richard Webber are still serving as pseudo mom and dad, respectively, on *Grey's*, doling out both parental advice and disappointed recriminations to the younger doctors—even though those original interns are now in their 40s.

And there's an argument to be had that Shonda Shows like *Scandal* and *How to Get Away with Murder* are carried by their "single mom" leads.

Creating a hodgepodge family of your own in a big city or on the job is a deeply Universal Fantasy. And man, do families blended by marriage resonate both on screen and in books.

Here are a just a few Created Family Universal Fantasies audiences love:

- a perfect kid in need of a good parent (single dad and mother romance, *Jerry Maguire*)
- a terrible kid in need of a good parent (nanny romance)
- *THE PARENT TRAP* (Seriously, I would read and watch every iteration of little kids setting up their parents for love if I could)
- lost twins reunited
- single woman longing for a child
- secret baby
- whoops pregnancy—really, she's pregnant with a love story!
- fur babies, horses, or any kind of reoccurring animal. Pets make for great family members—especially when they have your back like Gromit in *Wallace and Gromit*, Abu in the Disney version of

Aladdin, and the mice in Disney's version of *Cinderella*.
- work, school, and big city friend families (*Brooklyn 9-9*, *Grownish*, and *Friends* were preceded by *Barney Miller*, *Different World*, and *Living Single* for a reason —because this created families setup is BUTTER)

HOMEWORK

Now it's your turn. Think of one of your favorite ensemble TV shows and break down three of its characters. Who are they, and WHY do viewers love them?

BRIDGERTON: WORLD STUDY

Comp Shows: *Any historical series or other-worldly series. (ex. Outlander, Harry Potter, Game of Thrones, Steven Universe, etc.)*

If *Grey's Anatomy* ruins my Friday, the first season of this Shondaland show based on Julia Quinn's historical romance series ruined me for *days*. Like millions of readers and writers across America, I could not resist binging this beyond-delicious show.

Forget a diplomatic discussion with my husband about what we should watch that night once this launched—we were watching *THIS. THIS*, each and every night, until the entire tub of Universal Fantasy ice cream was consumed.

Now's a great time to talk about Americone Dream, my absolute favorite flavor of Ben & Jerry's ice cream.

Why do I adore this flavor so much, despite being lactose intolerant? Well, it has a familiar vanilla base with lots of things I also love packed inside, things like caramel and fudge-covered pieces of waffle cone. Oh my gosh, it is so yummy. And even better, because of my lactose intolerance —it is FORBIDDEN!

Bridgerton, for me, was Americone ice cream—guaranteed to tempt me away from work and packed with everything I liked from previous Shonda shows. Let's make a checklist, shall we?

Vanilla Ice Cream UF—check! I see you two leads who despise each other yet somehow conclude you can solve both of your problems with a FAKE RELATIONSHIP—a crazy popular trope because, as any dating reality show enthusiast could tell you, we lap up two veritable strangers doing all the stuff that real couples do until one of them proposes like *vanilla ice cream*.

Competition—check! All of these ladies are competing on the vicious Regency-era marriage market

Slay-All-Day—check! The characters, the walls—heck, even the credit-opening tree are all dressed to dazzle. Daphne Bridgerton, our heroine, is a "diamond of the first water" and seems to have been specially born and designed to wear an empire-waist dress. And the Duke of Hastings, our hero, is the tallest, richest, most handsome, and most eligible guy in every scene. Perfect series starter.

Irresistible ensemble of Comeback Kids—check! All the main ensemble characters have something to overcome. And they all have at least a dab of UF butter. There's….

- **Penelope Featherington**, the big, beautiful woman who'd rather study than go out on the marriage market—smart girl butter!
- **Lady Danbury**, the Duke's matchmaking honorary aunt who wants to help her nephew heal his childhood wounds through love—matchmaking auntie butter!
- The meme-riffic **Queen Charlotte**, who seeks utter control as she helplessly loses her husband—all hail the secretly suffering queen butter!

The list of UF goes on and on. But for the sake of brevity and study, we'll break down what makes the world of *Bridgerton* so utterly irresistible.

. . .

BRIDGERTON WORLD UF 1:

Opposite world. The Queen, The Ton, and the Wardrobe.

My third-grade teacher at the Lutheran school I attended for most of my elementary years used chapters of *The Lion, the Witch, and the Wardrobe* by C.S. Lewis as a reward for good behavior and classroom civility.

"I'd hate not to read that chapter," he'd warn when we got too loud or unruly. And here's the funny thing—that threat often worked. The '80s, man…

I'll never forget the rush of feeling in my chest the first time Lucy Pevensie, one of the book's main sibling characters, goes through the wardrobe and discovers a world nothing like her own. For me—and perhaps quite a few other students who glared at the bad apples when they lost us a chapter—visiting Narnia at the end of the school day represented stepping into another world.

Much of the charm of *Bridgerton* lies in the fact that it exists in a world completely opposite of our own.

The characters think, act, and dress differently than we do. Their dances were popularized outside of YouTube. They have entirely dissimilar priorities and pressures. I mean, how many of us have estates and legacies riding on our ability to produce an heir?

There are no microwaves or refrigerators in the world of *Bridgerton*. No Amazon delivery. No fast fashion. A seamstress must handcraft every dress. And the garments' arrival days to weeks after they're ordered is an event!

Even better, there are plenty of balls and galas to wear these lovely frocks to throughout something called a *season*.

This is a time when eligible women and men dress in their finest clothes to meet in person for the primary purpose of finding a possible marriage partner—not because they swept right on each other's picture and want to hook up.

This world doesn't look the same as ours. They wear things we cannot without being asked if we're attending a costume party. Their meals are prepared by a host of servants in the background. Their problems are nothing like our own.

Think of what your biggest problems were at 21. Now think of our main character, Daphne Bridgerton, who must either attract the attention of a suitable husband or suffer a lifetime of marriage to an odious baron who she doesn't remotely like.

Yeah, yeah, yeah, credit card debt—but look at this Lord Featherington fellow! What a pickle his habit of betting on backroom fisticuffs has gotten him in!

I can't convince my oldest kid to put down the manga and give a chapter book without pictures a go so that she has a chance of getting into college. But Baroness Featherington is exasperated with her daughter Penelope for caring more about books and her studies than securing a husband.

Regency Stars…they're just like us. Wait, no—they're NOTHING like us. All of these families are the exact opposite of relatable to most 21st-century humans. And viewers adore watching characters navigate problems that are not like theirs.

Remember, we modern-day humans are descended from hunter-gatherer nomads who eventually "discovered" the entire world.

Sometimes it was because they followed the wrong pack of animals and accidentally ended up on a whole new continent (*The Lion, the Witch, and the Wardrobe; Alice in Wonderland*). And sometimes it was because war, famine, weather, and/or destiny forced them to escape (*The Wizard of Oz, Harry Potter, Moana*).

Either way, Opposite Worlds tap into a primal part of us that loves to discover and experience places beyond our current reality.

And stories rich in world-building can feel like stepping through a wardrobe door into a wonderful new space.

Bonus Nightmare World UF: As delightful as so many of us found *Bridgerton*'s buttery take on the Regency era, we're also attracted to tales of dystopian futures where characters have to navigate problems and situations that are metastasized versions of our own. Think *Hunger Games, The Walking Dead,* or anything featuring a space war or alien takeover tales—whether it be a romance or a first contact sci-fi novel like Cixin Liu's *Three-Body Problem* trilogy.

BRIDGERTON WORLD UF 2:

Inclusion for the WIN. Make someone's fantasy come true.

As an African American woman who used to love historical romance but stopped reading them because they *never* included women who looked like me, the racially diverse casting of *Bridgerton* was nothing less than a fantasy come true. And I'll admit that I know way more about the American Revolution than I ever cared to understand because of the three times I've seen the stage play *Hamilton*.

I'm in the super fortunate position of having a target audience who almost over-appreciates me for simply writing books with Black heroines. So many of us grew up without seeing Black women cast in romantic roles between the pages of romance novels.

My generation will most likely remain forever grateful for the current sea change in books, and I get emails and comments nearly every day from appreciative readers. And some of the most heartfelt fan mail I've received has been for my bi-racial heroines—from Dominican, Filipina, and Afro-Latinx readers who were shocked and super pleased to see their culture featured in a leading role.

Human beings are social animals, and we love to be included—especially in spaces where we've never been featured.

I'll repeat that for the people who whine and moan about accuracy. ***Human beings are social animals, and we love to be included.***

I adored the *A Court of Thorns and Roses* series by Sarah J. Maas; she didn't make her fae race exclusively white. And this irresistible UF goes beyond skin color. One of my favorite IR reads of 2018 was *The Kiss Quotient* by Helen Hoang, a stellar and adorable romance featuring a white neurodivergent heroine and her Asian American love interest.

Inclusion is a simple but often overlooked way to serve readers beyond your target audience the fantasy they've been yearning for, and often these grateful readers become fans for life.

Remember, many readers of color won't buy into a world that doesn't ever bother to include them. But those who complained about *Bridgerton*'s accuracy watched to the very end of the first series—and will most likely show up for season two.

BRIDGERTON WORLD UF 3:

Rules, Scandal, Secrets, and Questions

Do you know what I love? Freedom. I love that I got to choose whom to marry and that I can live wherever I want and send my kids to non-segregated public schools and lay out my own career path.

In real life, the more freedom I enjoy, the better.

But in fantasy life?

Man, oh man, do I love a world with strict protocols and rules. That makes it way more delicious when characters break them. You skinny-dipping at an Airbnb—who cares? Daphne Bridgerton possibly being caught in the garden in the company of two fully clothed men? Gasp and Scandal!

In order to unlock that ever-popular punishment UF, rules must be broken. We all live in societies with laws and codes, so something thrills inside us when our character avatars break the rules and get punished. *You've been a bad girl, and now you must deal with the consequences.*

Special note on punishment: This also works for negative villains, and it's essential to make sure the punishment fits. Many *Game of Thrones* fans complained when a horrible, man-child ruler was poisoned without warning. Fans had spent seasons hating him, and his death came too fast—his punishment wasn't thrilling enough. In a later *GOT* season, another cruel ruler was thrown to the same dogs with whom he'd threatened one of the main characters to keep her frightened and cowed—a terrible death, to be sure. Fans cheered. His punishment was just right.

Broken rules are the main ingredient in scandal butter. And everything to do with scandal sells entertainment. Avoiding it, inviting it, overcoming it. So many media sites from the early millennium have come and gone. TMZ—the modern version of Lady Whistledown? It's still here.

Speaking of Whistledown, her identity is one of the many, many secrets and questions in which this world is steeped. Here are just a few from the first ten minutes of the first episode.

1. Who is Lady Whistledown?
2. Is Prudence Featherington's corset too tight?
3. Will Daphne Bridgerton find a suitable husband right away? How about True Love?
4. Has gaining Queen Charlotte's approval set a target on Daphne's back?
5. Will any of the Featherington girls make a match?

Well, you'll just have to stay in this world for ten more minutes to find out the answer to those questions.

But wait! While you get the answer to a few of those questions in the next bit, even more delicious questions and secrets pile on, including crushes, possibly pregnant country cousins, a diamond of the first water brought low. By the time the pilot is done, maybe it's technically possible to not watch the second episode. But I haven't met many people who have managed that feat.

Rules, Scandal, Secrets, and Questions are BUTTER. And even if readers only meant to peek into your world, adding these UFs will keep them locked in until the very end.

Now it's your turn. Recall a story with a world that sucked you right on in and write down three pieces of UF gold that made you want to stay for a while.

CHAPTER TEN
MODERN SAINTS OF ROMANCE: OUTLIERS

If you scan the Kindle Store Top 50 regularly, as I do, you'll find the usual suspects:

Traditional and indie writers who've established themselves as consistently good storytellers and who've managed to amass vast amounts of readers. You'll also find a ton of vanilla ice cream plots. Here are just a few from a casual scan done on the day I wrote this section:

- Fake engagement with hot neighbor.
- A spouse disappears, leaving behind a ton of secrets and a mystery that their partner must solve.
- Good Girl situations herself into a sex club and receives an indecent proposal.
- A no-strings-attached relationship develops into much more.
- An innocent submissive shifter needs the help and protection of a monstrous dominant shifter.

- A sports superstar finds himself stuck in a small town—and falling for a small-town girl.
- Not one, but two different bossholes in need of being torn down, fixed up, and rehabilitated by love. #HabitatForUniversalFantasy

Yay for these bestsellers. Audiences will never tire of vanilla ice cream—and honestly, I had to resist the urge to one-click a few of these even though my TBR is already overflowing.

But okay, okay, not everybody likes or wants to read or write vanilla ice cream. Some creators come up with more unusual content that readers have perhaps never seen before and/or weren't aware they would like. And these stories find their way to the top of the charts too.

Hey, what's that unfamiliar thing doing at the top of a chart?! Answer—GHEE!

However, that's not to say there's not a lot of Universal Fantasy going on in these surprise bestsellers too. If you break them down, they still have butter—it's just not the kind of butter we're used to. Let's call it ghee—a clarified butter that's awesome to cook with but that you might not have heard of or tried before.

In this section, we'll mine the Universal Fantasies in three books that made it to the top of their respective charts with ghee fantasies that resonated with audiences even though they didn't look like any of the other butter on the shelf.

First up…

PESTILENCE: BY LAUREN THALASSA

I am obsessed with this book.

I love the writing. I love the plot and the characters. And I especially love how the writer weaves so much Universal Fantasy ghee into her narrative. You absolutely can't put this book down.

The setup for this series is that the four horsemen of the apocalypse—Pestilence, War, Famine, and Death—come to earth to destroy all of humanity.

Pestilence comes to our firefighter heroine's town to spread disease. And after she draws the burnt matchstick, she's chosen as the person who will attempt to kill him.

But the thing is, Pestilence can't be killed. Thus, the preternaturally hot doomsday god ends up taking the heroine as a revenge prisoner as opposed to just inflicting her with the disease he's currently spreading throughout North America.

That's just a summary. But I highly, highly suggest you look at the actual description because it is a master class in writing a ghee-filled book description that makes readers think "I've never seen that before!" as they one-click.

Okay, check out how Universal Fantasy is incorporated into nearly every aspect of this setup.

First of all, this dude is one of the *FOUR HORSEMEN OF THE FREAKING APOCALYPSE*.

Talk about POWER Ghee. And he's definitely a fixer-upper! Chip and Joanna from *Fixer Upper*? Where you at? We got work to do!

Second of all, Sara has to defeat him to save her town and the human race from disease. Even before the pandemic, this was a high-stakes romance.

Saving something, someplace, someone, or someones you love is great motivation and a huge Universal Fantasy that powers pretty much every superhero blockbuster that has ever been made.

Third of all: This bitch can't be killed.

Now that is what writing books would call a FORMIDABLE VILLAIN.

This is why the Terminator is such an enduring antagonist.

And as quiet as it's kept, some of the most popular heroes in romance are the most formidable villains—mainly because readers want to see them redeemed.

Bully romances stay winning because of villain-heroes. And, I personally will one-click anything that so much as hints at a Hades-Persephone dynamic. Cruel and lusty alien overlords? Oh my gosh, not only do I co-write with Eve Vaughn a series featuring these villain-heroes, I have to resist the urge to read every new sci-fi romance that revolves around this kind of character.

That's a vanilla ice cream plot. But a horseman of the apocalypse—well, that was a flavor I never tried before.

Fourth of all: He kidnaps and imprisons her—ripping her out of her normal life. *Beauty and the Beast* UF represent. And he's going to *punish her*—ooh! HOT!

BUT even though this Supernatural Bully is being mean to Sara, he really likes her. And although the hero is incensed at Sara for shooting him and setting him on fire, he can't stay that way because she's so damn irresistible—cue that primal preen.

These are all GREAT Universal Fantasies, many of which we discussed during the *Beauty and the Beast* portion.

Frankly, the author could have stopped the description here and gotten my enemies-to-lovers one-click. But then she mentions a sacrifice of the heart in the last paragraph of her book description.

I like to refer to this as a dog-whistle fantasy—in a good way, not a political or horrible one. I call it this because, the real Universal Fantasy is not stated outright, but somehow, we all understand what's about to go down.

This dude cannot be beaten with physical force.

Sacrificing her heart basically means The Power of the Magical Pussy is required to take down our formidable villain hero.

I won't do a history lesson here. I'll just say that this taps into a long-held Universal Fantasy of women being able to take down powerful men through sex and love.

So that's a breakdown of a book description by a then-new-to-me author on whom I decided to take a chance based on her book description—and the fact that she was ranked so high in the Amazon store.

Whether or not your book has thousands of reviews, I suggest making a routine of going through your category's Top 50 on whatever platform you prefer regularly.

Read the book descriptions and see if you can identify the Universal Fantasies for the books that are not necessarily supposed to be there.

Here are a couple of other books by then-new-to-me authors whose ghee-filled situations made me one-click.

***The Air He Breathes* by Brittany Cherry:** A widower who loses his wife and son in a car accident meets a widowed single mom who lost her husband in a car accident. As a happily married mom of three, this set-up struck me as particularly horrific. But I gave it a chance for the same reason I keep tuning into *Grey's Anatomy*. I wanted to see these two *suffering* and *wounded* people *come back* and *fix* each other with love. Ghee!

***The Kiss Quotient* by Helen Hoang:** As an awkward person, I immediately one-clicked this romance when I discovered the heroine was even more awkward than I am. Also, I'd never read or seen a romance featuring a female lead on the autism spectrum. So I, like so many others, was immediately curious to see how her romance would play out.

Again, a heroine who's never or rarely been spotlighted before can be fantastic UF ghee. Readers who aren't in her situation want to taste this new dish, and readers who are feel *included*.

I also love when themes like achieving racial justice, overcoming mental illness, beating cancer, and thriving with disabilities find their way into romance novels.

These are things we dream about in both fantasy and real life.

Universal Fantasies borne out of social justice or frustrations with the real world are GOLD.

This is why revisionist movies like Quentin Tarantino's *Django Unchained*, in which a powerful Black man saves his enslaved wife, and revisionist miniseries like Ryan Murphy's *Hollywood*, which reimagines the dismantlement of the sexist, racist, homophobic Hollywood Golden Age studio system, attracted so many fans despite not being historically accurate.

And let's take a look at the surprise Netflix hit, *The Queen's Gambit*, based on the Walter Tevis novel of the same name. It's a masterclass in ghee fantasy, including…

- **Getting really good at chess.** Chess set sales famously rose after the release of this miniseries. I think a lot of us low-key wanted to do this.
- **Earning a mother's approval through your talent and making a few of that parent's dreams come true.** Oh, man, as a daughter whose mom died when I was 19, I could not *not* over-invest in this relationship.
- **Slay-All-Day wardrobe**. '50s edition!
- **Opposite World…of chess.** I knew nothing about the world of high-stakes chess before this miniseries, and I became obsessed with it. This strange opposite world is also what makes me one-click the latest graphic novel volume of C.S. Pacat's *Fence* series—which is, yes, set in the world of epic epee fighting—as soon as it comes up for pre-order.
- **A *woman* gets a karate kid *makeover* in a mostly male sport.** My competition avatar was ALL IN. I played chess SO HARD on my couch.

- **All your exes happily work together for your benefit**. I mean…it never occurred to me that this would be nice—but wouldn't it be nice? (At least for some of us. My editor let me know that this idea fills her with cringe. Lol!)

HOMEWORK

Okay, time for more homework.

Recall the last bestseller that surprised you. If you didn't particularly like this story yourself, even better!

As a darkish and smutty romance writer, I don't particularly love light and sweet rom coms. But reading them never fails to introduce UFs *I can still use*—more on that later.

Read the description for whatever surprise bestseller you pick out and see if you can suss out at least one or two of its ghee UFs. Believe me, they all have at least one. Ghee is the secret sauce of unusual bestsellers.

Note: Not every surprise bestseller has a stellar blurb. If you can't figure out the attraction from the book description, go to the reviews. Let readers tell you why they lapped it up.

PART THREE

YOUR STEP-BY-STEP ACTION PLAN FOR INFUSING UF BUTTER INTO YOUR WRITING AND MARKETING

HOW TO INTEGRATE UNIVERSAL FANTASY INTO EVERYTHING YOU DO

If you've done all the homework, you should understand Universal Fantasy so thoroughly that this last part will be a breeze.

If you're like me and NEVER do the homework—like, even when you were in actual school—then this is the perfect time to practice all the things you've just read about before the **BIG TEST**.

Joking. There is no big test. The plans and advice offered in this part of the book are suggestions and in no way prescriptive. Take what you need; Frankenstein it into your own system. Use the UF however you like. You can close the book right now if you want.

But I like recipes. So here are a few, just in case you do too.

CHAPTER ELEVEN
UNIVERSAL FANTASY IS THE SECRET BUTTER SAUCE— SERIOUSLY, PUT IT IN EVERYTHING

Okay, let's finally come back to *Her Viking Wolf* and figure out why the book with the crappy cover sold.

It's often hard to figure out what makes your book delicious. That's why we've just spent loads of pages delving into Universal Fantasy through properties across the entertainment spectrum.

In *Her Viking Wolf's* case, it turned out that the book sold—even with a crappy cover—because I'd unwittingly tapped into a few powerful Universal Fantasies with my description.

Let's read the *Viking Wolf* description. And we'll take the following action steps while we do so:

1. Clear your mind of expectations and cynicism.
2. Pay attention to the parts that spark something inside of you.

3. Pay special attention to anything that makes you imagine yourself in the same situation.
4. If you're not a fan of paranormal, think of someone who would enjoy this book and think about why.
5. Write down a list of things that would make you or someone else want to read this book. Mine its Universal Fantasies.

Okay, here's the description:

When Chloe Adams was four, her shiftless shifter parents abandoned her on the side of the road.

But now she's reinvented herself as a DIY domestic goddess, and she's engaged to the hottest alpha in Colorado—that is until a large, red-haired, time-traveling Viking werewolf shows up to claim her as his fated mate.

Wait, what?!?!

WARNING: This smoking-hot romance contains jaw-dropping twists and turns, sizzling sex scenes, and nothing less than the adventure of a lifetime. It should only be read by those who like their Vikings red haired and red hot!

That's the description.

Were you able to figure out why this book sold?

> Here's the answer…**a woman who was wounded by her parents** is shocked **when a beast of a Viking** shows up in her time and **pulls her out of her ill-fitting life** by **claiming her as his fated mate**.

I didn't realize it back then, but that's basically four Universal Fantasies happening in one description.

But the winning fantasy turned out to be that red-headed *beast* of a Viking—doing what the romance novel version of Vikings have been doing so well for decades and decades—storming into a lead's life and *ripping her out of it*.

And as for the resulting ad that's still going after three years —it just WORKS.

Check it out…

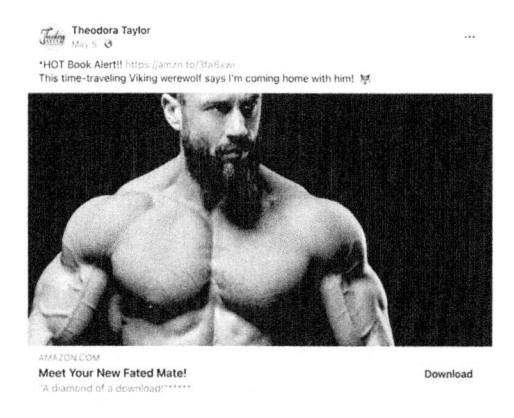

> **Theodora Taylor**
> May 5
>
> *HOT Book Alert!! https://am.zn.to/3fa8xwi
> This time-traveling Viking werewolf says I'm coming home with him! 🐺
>
> AMAZON.COM
> **Meet Your New Fated Mate!**   Download
> "A diamond of a download!"*****

So, SO simple.

It took me longer to find the right models on Shutterstock than it did for me to make that ad.

Done right, your central Universal Fantasy will *easily* sell books for you.

Which is why I always like to do some warm-up marketing before I begin new projects. Meet me in the next chapter to talk more about that.

CHAPTER TWELVE
BACKLIST BEFORE YOU FRONTLIST

I'm a highly future-oriented person. If you know anything about Gallup Strengths, I'm a No. 1 Futuristic. That means I'm always looking forward and almost never backward.

However, before beginning a new project, I often find it helpful to set up an ad campaign for one of my backlist series. If the backlist series is connected to or feeds into my upcoming series, yippee! If not, no worries; all new readers are good readers. Either way, I spend some time connecting with my potential audience before I spend a ton more time writing a book by myself.

When I wanted to highlight my bestselling Chinese mafia romance series, *Ruthless Triad*, I heavily promoted *Ruthless Tycoons*, a series that had ended with a delicious teaser for *Triad*. *Tycoons* was a great series for me to revisit because I'd initially marketed it before figuring out Universal Fantasy. So we'll do this exercise using that campaign as an example.

Your chosen book should be a first in series, too—preferably one that did well during its initial release. If you don't write in series, simply choose your previous bestselling book.

First, mine 3–5 Universal Fantasies for your book. For *HOLT: Her Ruthless Billionaire*, the first book in my *Ruthless Tycoons* series, I came up with:

1. **Opposite sides of the tracks first love.** Scion falls hard for a little nobody—primal preen.
2. **Bitter and/or tragic breakup.** Oh my gosh, for me and many other readers, this is like watching a beautiful piece of artwork break in two —especially if it's a True Love Match. If you've ever listened to that song "The Origin of Love" from *Hedwig and the Angry Inch*, that's the same feeling readers have in their chests after a tragic breakup. And we just have to keep reading until these two are *fixed* and glued back together.
3. **Powerful, arrogant CEO.** I smell a bosshole who needs to be *taken down* and *fixed* by love!
4. **Punishment disguised as a job.** My powerful and extremely bitter CEO forces his ex to become a nanny for his emotionally dysregulated son, therefore ripping her out of her boring life. At the time of writing this book, I'd read plenty of single dad romances, but none with an ex-girlfriend who's forced to take a job as a nanny for her ex's neurodivergent kid who truly needs her. GHEE!
5. **My heroine has a HUGE SECRET** that compels her to make an *indecent proposal deal* with her new boss to let her go in exchange for a few months of no strings-attached sex.

Funnily enough, before figuring out Universal Fantasy, I didn't even realize my UF No. 4 was butter. UFs Nos. 1, 2, and 3 had already instinctually gone into my book description, and UF No. 5 would be a spoiler. But upon second look at my original ads for this series, I realized that I was missing a huge opportunity by not including No. 4 in the marketing campaign.

Here are the final ad results.

> What Holt Calson wants, Holt Calson gets. And unfortunately, what my extremely bitter billionaire ex wants now is red hot, sexy revenge.
>
> Amazon US: http://amzn.to/2z5wiiR
>
> OH. MY. GAWD!
> ★★★★★
>
> DISPLAYURL.COM
> **Worst breakup EVER**
> ON SALE FOR 0.99—LIMITED TIME ON...
> USE APP

ORIGINAL AD

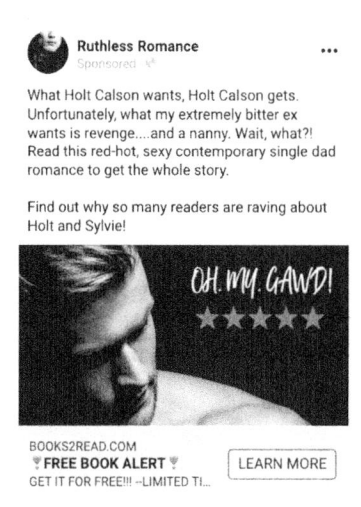

> **Ruthless Romance**
> Sponsored
>
> What Holt Calson wants, Holt Calson gets. Unfortunately, what my extremely bitter ex wants is revenge....and a nanny. Wait, what?! Read this red-hot, sexy contemporary single dad romance to get the whole story.
>
> Find out why so many readers are raving about Holt and Sylvie!
>
> *OH. MY. GAWD!* ★★★★★
>
> BOOKS2READ.COM
> 🏆 **FREE BOOK ALERT** 🏆   [LEARN MORE]
> GET IT FOR FREE!!! –LIMITED TI...

AD ON UF

Adding the bosshole single dad in need of a nanny twist to the extremely bitter ex butter made this book even more appealing to cold readers—readers who'd never heard of me or this book. By looking at this ad, they knew that this bosshole would get taken down—and what he needed.

Bonus note for me: While doing this exercise, I realized that I could add "—and a nanny for his out-of-control son" to the next campaign and most likely get even more clicks. I am a sucker for kids receiving the nanny (soon-to-be mother) they deserve and need.

Now your turn. If you have an original ad to compare your new one to, even better. If not, no worries. Simply write copy that incorporates your story's tastiest UF gold.

Extra Tip: I love making a Facebook ad, then distilling my most potent UF into one for Amazon as well.

CHAPTER THIRTEEN
OUTLINING FOR THE WIN: HOW TO GET RIGHT WITH UNIVERSAL FANTASY BEFORE YOU WRITE

Write the book description before you write the book.

Arghh! This is one of those pieces of advice that used to frustrate me because before I learned how to mine UF gold, I didn't know how to implement it.

I mean, sure, it makes sense to have some idea of what you're offering readers before you get to writing. But I often didn't know why a story was delicious until I was done writing it—sometimes not even then.

So, before UF, I had a lot of anemic book descriptions kicking around that were a bunch of "what happened" sentences glued together by prayers and hope.

But now it breaks down rather simply for me:

Step 1: Outline your story generally in one run-on sentence.

Example: A nerdy Indian girl with a recently deceased father and John McEnroe for an inner voice starts her sophomore year of high school determined to shake off old labels and finally lose her virginity to her popular crush. (*Never Have I Ever*)

Step 2: Outline your book with one sentence for each part of a 3-act story structure plot—or whatever kind of plot you prefer.

If you're looking for a great example of this step, please check out Michelle Schusterman's Fast Outlining method on YouTube. I discovered it when I needed to outline a really good book *fast* to meet a pre-order deadline less than a month away, and I've used her super simple method for every book since.

Step 3: Outline your story with one sentence for each chapter/episode.

Spoiler alert for the below if you haven't yet seen the fantastic Netflix series, *Never Have I Ever*. But seriously, if that's the case, why haven't you?!

I nearly included a Modern Saints section on Mindy Kaling shows (*Never Have I Ever*, the *Four Weddings and a Funeral* reboot series, *The Office*, and *The Mindy Project*—but decided it would be too much. She excels at the "Just as I Am" Universal Fantasy. This is when women who are both non-mainstream beautiful and cringy—you know, like the vast majority of women on the planet—manage to attract worthy guys because of their complicated and unique personalities. I *adore* this UF in both fantasy and real-life—I consider myself a "Just as I Am" woman and try to aggressively be myself. See *Bridget Jones Diary* by Helen Fielding and the wonderful television series *Crazy Ex-Girlfriend* for other modern examples.

But enough fangirling. Here's your example episode/chapter sentence breakdown:

Episode One: Determined to finally become cool after overcoming a literally paralyzing trauma reaction to her father's sudden death, Devi asks the most popular guy in school to have sex with her, and he says yes!

Episode Two: Devi experiences a setback on her goal to becoming cool when her sexual assignation with Paxton goes awkwardly and ends with an argument, but then Paxton apologizes to Devi for the misunderstanding and finds himself intrigued by her one-of-a-kind personality.

Step 4: Outline your book way more specifically with a beat-by-beat breakdown for each chapter. This is exactly like Step 3, but every scene gets its own sentence.

Step 5: Add a Universal Fantasy under each chapter breakdown.

Shortly after I figured out that Universal Fantasy was a powerful tool, I started writing the *Alien Overlord* series with Eve Vaughn under the pen name Taylor Vaughn.

Eve and I are both IR writers, and we were both new to the alien romance genre. Our readers never asked us for this collaboration, and a few of them were adamant in their dislike of alien romance altogether.

But *His to Claim*, the first entry in our alien romance series, went on to earn more than any other book in either of our paranormal catalogs in its first six months.

The first three books of the series, which we launched in March 2019, earned over six figures by the end of December 2019. The audio version of the first book earned out in less than 30 days! And the first book continues to convert readers and read-through like gangbusters.

Not bad for a new pen name!

I'm going to use the first book in the series to explain Step 5 and to illustrate how we employed Universal Fantasy to sell the book to a mass audience *and* our core groups of readers, many of whom claimed to HATE alien romance.

Step 5 Examples:
Adding a Universal Fantasy to each scene.

PARAGRAPH EXAMPLE:

Honestly, I don't usually put this much detail in my chapter breakdowns. This one was written out purely because Eve is a pantser (advice for that kind of writer coming up in the next chapter). so this outline had to be understood by both of us.

HIS TO CLAIM

After her sister dies trying to escape the Xalthurians, Kira [the heroine] gets in a physical fight with the leader of the alien horde, who turns out to be his race's future king. Immediately turned on and intrigued by her, the alien prince picks her up by the neck, sees that she's not of breeding age yet, and vows to come back for her in two years when she is…before dropping her in the dirt.

Universal Fantasies: worthy villain hero beast fixer-upper in need of taming, popular/rich guy picks you, bully is cruel to you but really likes you, future punishment.

I highly recommend the paragraph(s) method if you're co-writing or on deadline and/or want to write fast and need to be super clear. Because I switch up outlines, according to the book, I'll include samples of each kind of outline with books other than *His to Claim* after this paragraph one.

BULLET POINT EXAMPLE:

GOLDIE AND THE THREE BEARS (A CONTEMPORARY REVERSE HAREM)

1. Goldie's car breaks down in the Wisconsin woods while she is pregnant and on the run from abusive ex-cop BF.
2. Walks to try to find a gas station.
3. Too far. But when she comes back, car gone!!!
4. Finds cabin in the woods.
5. Makes herself a meal.
6. Sees three rooms—one with an overly huge bed, a closet under the stairs with a bed jammed inside, and a room with an en suite bathroom and a regular-sized bed.
7. Takes shower. Falls asleep naked in the just-right bed.

Universal Fantasies: shelter from the storm/cold, struggling heroine, comeback kid, familiar fairytale retold

ONE-SENTENCE EXAMPLE:

Prologue - *Phantom: Her Ruthless Fiancé* (the last book in the *Triad* series. I'd been thinking about it for *years*—this story barely required outlining)

Phantom, a coarse and violent triad dragon, shows up in Dr. Olivia's office to intimidate her out of asking any more questions about the intern who abruptly quit—falls in instalove with her instead.

Universal Fantasy(s): Instalove, fated love, bully becomes teddy bear for you

Main point: write the scene out in as many words as you want, then establish at least one Universal Fantasy that would keep readers swiping past that scene. Move on to the next scene and do the same thing. Wash and repeat until you have a delicious *and* nutritious outline.

Perhaps not shockingly, after we had our outline chock-filled with UFs, it was way easier for Eve and me to come up with a book description that would attract readers outside of our original target audience who were really on the fence about this book.

This leads us directly into…

Step 6: *NOW* write your book description.

This turned out to be great advice—especially for a co-write. Writing and agreeing to our description beforehand ensured Eve and I were on the same page as we wrote.

But why stop there? There's one more step that will ensure that you're writing something that will be easy to sell…

CHAPTER FOURTEEN
AD BEFORE YOU WRITE

This is a terrific place to revisit the simple description of Universal Fantasy.

THE

REASON

OR

REASONS*

PEOPLE

ENJOY

YOUR

STORY

*You only need one really good Universal Fantasy to sell a book, but of course, the more the

SELLIER

This means that the foundation of most highly converting ads, blurbs, back cover descriptions, and stellar reviews is simply explaining to or showing your readers

THE REASON OR REASONS THEY WILL ENJOY YOUR BOOK.

Let's get clear here.

Because while this sounds simple on the surface, this is what trips up a lot of writers when it comes to marketing bestsellers:

You are NOT telling readers why they *should* read your book.

You are NOT telling your readers why your book is "good."

You are NOT saying to readers, "Trust me. I made a list once with another book, so this book might be good too."

NO!

With your marketing materials—which, by the way, include the first few chapters of your work and your heavily marketed series starters—you are **SHOWING** readers why they will enjoy your book.

And by ENJOY, I mean be ENTERTAINED for hours for less than the cost of a venti pumpkin spice latte at Starbucks. By the way, whenever writers balk at readers who aren't willing to buy a book for less than a Starbucks drink from an author they don't know, I always say…

**I'm willing to pay more
for a Starbucks drink
than a book by a random author
I've never heard of
because I KNOW
my venti pumpkin spice latte
WON'T SUCK!**

By incorporating Universal Fantasy into your marketing materials, you're basically assuring readers that their experience with your book WON'T SUCK.

And, if you can create a compelling Facebook ad *before* you start writing your next book, then you're setting yourself up for a better seller.

Prior to putting together the soft launch of my Universal Fantasy presentation, I'd written the third book in my *Brothers Nightwolf* werewolf shifter trilogy.

It was a long-awaited trilogy finisher and highly anticipated by my fans. And it had been teased well in previous books. The novel involved one-of-a-kind characters, a ton of funny situations, and an incredible Love-Over-70 B-story.

There were just two problems…

That "there's something wrong" feeling plagued me throughout the construction of the book, which not only made it hard to write with joy and certainty but also caused me lots of delays due to anxiety and dread. Even worse, when I finally finished writing it, I couldn't figure out how to market it.

It was a perfectly nutritious book in the end, thanks to good craft and editing—technically awesome. But I couldn't think of anything non-spoilery to say in the Facebook ads, other than "Hey! Opposites Attract! Hop on it!"

This let me know that my hardcore fans would love this book, but new readers wouldn't be able to get into it. I launched the book, and, sure enough, longtime fans of the series loved it, but it was my poorest seller of the year.

I still love that story, but I never wanted to find myself in that place again.

So now, if I can't come up with ad copy that employs a specific Universal Fantasy from my to-be-written novel, I either rework the outline or think twice about writing that story.

These ads for *His to Claim* were EASY to think up. Before typing the first word of that book, I knew that these Universal Fantasies would attract the new readers we needed to make this launch successful and convince our contemporary readers to give this alien romance a try.

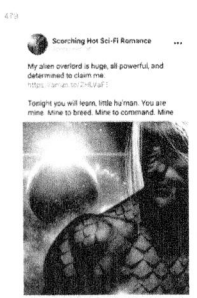

Universal Fantasies Included in these Amazon and Facebook ads:

—Banging a Beast

—Getting punished because you've been bad

—A Formidable Villain Hero

—Abuse of Power

His to Claim was the first book I did this for, and it's my bestselling non-contemporary to date. As of this writing, Eve and I receive messages on every separate new release we put out, asking when we'll finish this series. And even readers who hated it seemed to be unable to stop consuming it.

Some of my favorite *His to Claim* reviews are one-stars SCREAMING about how absolutely wrong the book is and how when the reader got to the end of the book, they had to come write a one-star review to WARN others about this terrible book.

As a writer who never finishes books she doesn't find compelling, all I can say to those readers is thank you for the full read of a book that was enrolled in the Kindle Unlimited program—which pays by page reads.

I know Universal Fantasy did its job because instead of not finishing the book they supposedly hated, they made sure I was paid in full for a story that OUTRAGED them.

Love it!

CHAPTER FIFTEEN
#CHARACTERGOALS: USING UF TO CREATE IRRESISTIBLE CHARACTERS

This is a step that can go anywhere in your process or get skipped altogether, depending on your relationship with your characters.

Some characters—like Phantom and Olivia from the last book in my *Triad* series came to me so fully formed, I didn't have to bother with this step. But some characters, like Kel D'Rek and Kyra from *His to Claim*, were simply blocks of character wood inside a crafted situation until we carved them out and breathed some life into them.

I love me some plots, so, in an ideal project sprint, this step comes after I've put together my outline. But I'll admit to sometimes not employing it until I get stuck—and sometimes not until I get character notes from my editor that I'm not sure how to solve!

On the flip side, this step is my first stop when I have absolutely nothing in mind for two side characters. Quite a few of my bestsellers started with me figuring out my MCs (Main Characters) and then plugging what I had into an awesome character-first plotting system such as Lisa Cron's Story Genius book, or Abbie Emmons's 3-Act Story Structure YouTube Tutorials.

However you want to use this simple UF Character Development trick, it's here for you. Please feel free to make it your own. I write darkish cisgender m/f romance. So, Character A is always the woman and Character B is always the man. But label and pronoun it however you want.

Character A:

Description:

GMC (Goal, Motivation, Conflict):

UF Relatable Butter:

UF Butter:

UF Ghee:

What will falling in love solve for her?

Character B:

Description:

GMC:

UF Villain Butter:

UF Wound Butter:

UF Ghee:

What will falling in love solve for him?

Please note that this Character UF breakdown is very personal to me and my universal audience.

As a non-traditional writer in a non-traditional relationship, I always want a bit of ghee in my characters—otherwise I don't enjoy writing them. I love but could never write Olivia Pope myself—so I always add a pat of relatable butter in my heroine's ingredient list.

I'm the kind of fan who crushed on Skeletor instead of He-Man when she was a kid. And, as someone who lost her mother when she was 19, I find it hard to be interested in anyone without some character-developing wound in their past in both real and fantasy life. So, all of my male leads include pats of villain and wound butters.

This is all to say, I have specific kinds of butter I like to work with for my books. You can use whatever kind of butter you want, and feel free to add your own preferred adjectives to your butter descriptions.

But if you want readers to engage with your characters in ways that make them dress up like your heroine for Halloween or take to Facebook groups to declare your hero their Book Boyfriend and offer to fight anyone else who tries to claim him, make sure to infuse your characters with UF butter.

For the purpose of this example, we'll use the *Victor* trilogy, my bestselling contemporary series of all time to fill out this character grid.

Character A: Dawn

Description: Half-Korean, Half-Black teenager living with her parents in Japan. As a fat bi-racial person in Japan, she has low self-esteem and receives zero attention from guys. She is sure her last year of high school will be as romance-free as the first three.

GMC: She wants to apply to her dream art school but feels super-conflicted about it because her parents want her to become a doctor. When a mysterious and crazy hot Chinese mafia prince offers her a job as his tutor, she takes it. He makes her super nervous and she soon falls in crush with him, but how could a guy like him like a girl like her?

UF Relatable Butter: Low self-esteem and plus sized—so relatable.

UF Butter: Fish-out-of-water in Japan. Through Dawn's eyes, we get to experience another world without a 10-hour-plus flight and a language barrier.

UF Ghee: She knows ASL (American Sign Language) and therefore can teach and communicate with the mute hero better than pretty much any other girl her age. True Love Match quality.

What will falling in love solve for her? She'll gain self-esteem and the bravery to follow her dreams.

Character B: Victor

Description: High school-age son of a powerful Hong Kong crimelord dragon.

GMC: Sees sweet girl dancing and signing in ASL with her Hard of Hearing brother on the dance floor at one of his father's nightclubs. Wants to learn her version of sign language to get closer to her—he only knows CSL (Chinese Sign Language). So he hires her on as a tutor. But after he does that, he doesn't know how to tell her he has a crush on her.

UF Villain Butter: Dangerous, violent, and will do any evil thing to help and protect Dawn.

UF Butter: Most powerful high schooler in this world. He commands everyone around him, even the adults. But he's a teddy bear for Dawn.

UF Wound Ghee: Mute due to a wound from a terrible, secret backstory. So must express himself through sign language.

What will falling in love solve for him? Meeting and falling for Dawn introduces a warm, sweet love into his cold and harsh world and puts him on a path to healing and redemption.

Please note that this exercise also works for side characters. Nothing earns you emails like "When is X Character's story going to come out?" like making sure X has at least a few dabs of UF butter in their cameo.

But enough pre-gaming, let's get to writing with UF!

CHAPTER SIXTEEN
RULES FOR WRITING YOUR BETTER SELLER:
USING UF TO MAKE WRITING YOUR STORY WAY LESS CONFUSING

Alright, I know there are probably at least a few pantsers reading this. Just to let you know, it can be fun to mine for Universal Fantasies while writing as opposed to formally identifying them beforehand. And while I hate having to do page one rewrites when a character gives me a major piece of information I didn't have prior to writing, that's a fun part of the book's creation story for some writers.

This section is for every writer on the pre-planning spectrum.

As you're writing, keep in mind…

RULE 1:
Every Scene and Every Chapter Should Have at Least One Universal Fantasy

If you're not outlining, I suggest pausing at the end of each scene you write and making a mental note about what Universal Fantasies came up in that scene.

If you can't think of any, then that scene probably needs major edits.

As a rule of thumb, people should be able to identify at least one of your Universal Fantasies from chapter one. And each scene after that should either be setup for a Universal Fantasy or have some kind of Universal Fantasy playing out.

If a scene doesn't involve a Universal Fantasy, it shouldn't be a scene.

It should be a line or two—a paragraph at most. Otherwise, it's not enjoyable—it's just information. Which could lead to boredom.

And, oh my gosh, don't be boring!

RULE 2:
Every Scene Should Be Bestie and/or Instagram Worthy

Right now, you might be saying something like—but, I love long, hot showers. I enjoy a cup of coffee and a good, long interior monologue think in the morning.

How do you know my scene in which a character wakes up and then thinks for pages and pages about her new job and current life situation while grabbing a long shower and some coffee afterward isn't butter?

Or maybe you're not so confident. Maybe you, like me, honestly have trouble telling if a few of your scenes are interesting and enjoyable?

Even during my playwright days, I often didn't know I lost my audience with a long riff until I, well, lost them. Ugh! Nothing like getting negative feedback from actors who would go on to headline movies and TV shows. Still shuddering.

And I have a super short attention span, so often advice like "If you're bored, they're bored" doesn't apply to me. I am so easily bored, and most often it's during the really important parts, such as the last action sequence where my hero and heroine physically fight some obstacle for their love.

So, here are my two super-simple "Is this boring?" test questions:

Would you call your best friend about it?

I talk to my best friend every weekday. To be honest, our conversations are pretty mundane. But there are certain things I call her about as soon as they happen.

Like, "Hey, we just sold our house!"

OR

"Hey! I just saw Beyoncé and Jay-Z on the stairs at the Neues Museum in Berlin!"

But I don't call her out of the blue to tell her that I took a shower, worked out, thought long and hard about the new book I was starting, ate oatmeal for breakfast, or any of the many mundane things I do throughout the sixteen hours of my waking day to get from points A to P.

Yet, I'm always seeing long scenes like this in books!

Nothing makes me DNF a book faster than having to slog through a character getting up, taking a shower, and making a bowl of cereal while talking to her roommate who doesn't have a particularly interesting job.

That is so, so boring.

Here's an even easier way to deduce whether a scene should be cut down or cut altogether:

> **If you were or knew this character, would you post about what happened in this scene on social media?**

That Beyoncé story is true, by the way. It was so exciting, I not only called my best friend afterward, but I made a post about it on Facebook.

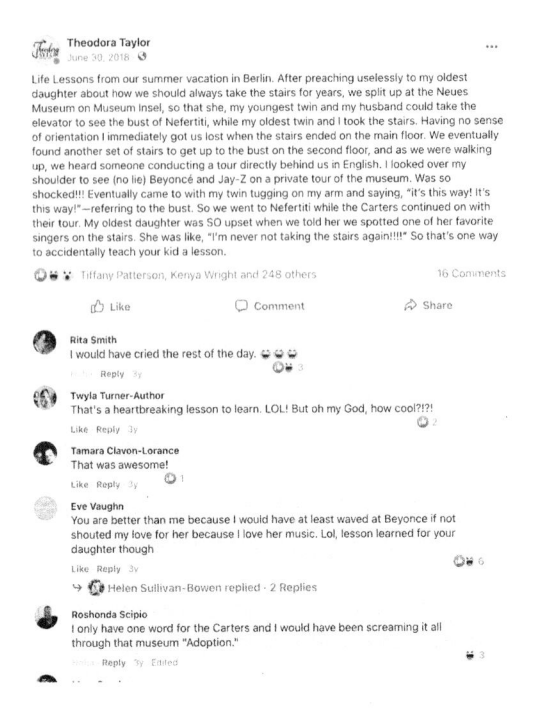

> **Theodora Taylor**
> June 30, 2018
>
> Life Lessons from our summer vacation in Berlin. After preaching uselessly to my oldest daughter about how we should always take the stairs for years, we split up at the Neues Museum on Museum Insel, so that she, my youngest twin and my husband could take the elevator to see the bust of Nefertiti, while my oldest twin and I took the stairs. Having no sense of orientation I immediately got us lost when the stairs ended on the main floor. We eventually found another set of stairs to get up to the bust on the second floor, and as we were walking up, we heard someone conducting a tour directly behind us in English. I looked over my shoulder to see (no lie) Beyoncé and Jay-Z on a private tour of the museum. Was so shocked!!! Eventually came to with my twin tugging on my arm and saying, "it's this way! It's this way!"—referring to the bust. So we went to Nefertiti while the Carters continued on with their tour. My oldest daughter was SO upset when we told her we spotted one of her favorite singers on the stairs. She was like, "I'm never not taking the stairs again!!!!" So that's one way to accidentally teach your kid a lesson.
>
> Tiffany Patterson, Kenya Wright and 248 others — 16 Comments
>
> Like — Comment — Share
>
> **Rita Smith**
> I would have cried the rest of the day. 😭😭😭
> Reply · 3y
>
> **Twyla Turner-Author**
> That's a heartbreaking lesson to learn. LOL! But oh my God, how cool?!?!
> Like · Reply · 3y
>
> **Tamara Clavon-Lorance**
> That was awesome!
> Like · Reply · 3y
>
> **Eve Vaughn**
> You are better than me because I would have at least waved at Beyonce if not shouted my love for her because I love her music. Lol, lesson learned for your daughter though
> Like · Reply · 3y
> ↳ Helen Sullivan-Bowen replied · 2 Replies
>
> **Roshonda Scipio**
> I only have one word for the Carters and I would have been screaming it all through that museum "Adoption."
> Reply · 3y · Edited

And the post got a ton of clicks on it! Because it was *interesting*.

If you want your writing to be exciting and enjoyable, make sure that even the food descriptions are worthy of being posted on Instagram.

You don't want to give your readers a bowl of cereal eaten over pages of interior monologue. You want to give them a fantasy meal they can taste.

So even for the small stuff, always keep Universal Fantasy in the back of your head.

However…

RULE 3:
Butter to Taste

Listen, I'm from Missouri and raised by parents who both grew up in Mississippi before coming north with the Great Migration.

So I adore lard. I chow down on heavy and rich romance, and I put huge sticks of butter in almost everything I write. But trust, there are plenty of bestsellers that don't use as much butter as me and some of my faves.

It's up to each writer to decide how much butter they want to put in.

I love describing meals. I do not take a page to do it like J.K. Rowling does. A little butter or a lot of butter is fine.

And for some Universal Fantasies, you can even make it your own kind of butter.

I'm a huge fan of oleo--and not just because that alternative word for margarine shows up in crossword puzzles, like, all of the time.

Oleo is what I call using the UF energy from one genre or category for a totally opposite category or genre.

Examples might include...

An age gap romance dynamic between two over-40s lovers. Quiet as it's kept, some grown women fantasize about traditionally Age Gap romance UFs like getting coached and dominated out of their sexual innocence—especially if the heroine's an unappreciated divorcee comeback kid who's making over her life and character. So I do love a male MC who's willing to do the same things an Age Gap MC would to someone his own age. Oleo!

A small-town romance set on another planet with big blue aliens—I see you, Ruby Dixon.

A colorful ensemble sitcom that takes place in the afterlife and tackles huge philosophical questions. Not to be that cliche reviewer, but I would honestly give *The Good Place* 10 stars if I could.

I adore oleo books.

So don't be afraid to play around and make every book your own.

Which brings us to rule 4…

RULE 4:
Moral to Taste

At the end of my talks, I tend to get questions about shameful UF butter. These are the fantasies that some authors and readers will shame you about.

Some currently hot market examples of seemingly shameful fantasies that attract a lot of outraged one-star reviews are…

alien romance

daddy/Little romance

and academy reverse harem bully romance

The people who don't like those kinds of books yell much louder than the ones who quietly and happily enter fantasy worlds where they can

- have sex with a conquering alien,
- get treated like a little girl by a daddy figure,
- become the object of obsession for a cruel harem of high school boys

These books *sell*. And that's because they provide a safe place to experience this fantasy without real-life commitment.

I'm super happy I've gotten to kill that horrible guy who really deserved it, run a super-successful meth business in New Mexico, and, check me out, *eclipsed my mom*. Not only have I won more awards than she, but early onset dementia also hasn't come for me.

This is all to say, my love of *Dexter*, *Breaking Bad*, and *Grey's Anatomy* has allowed me to experience the fantasy without transferring it to my real life.

But the truth is, if Dr. Who invited me to travel with them throughout the universe in real life, I'd be, like, "No. I'm quite squeamish, and I don't like my odds for not dying while in the company of a so-called doctor who can't fully explain the questionable science they're using to power their vehicle and adventures."

I do, however, like watching a television show about these adventures from the safety of my couch. And though I've never had an IRL bosshole, I will continue telling them off in my head until the day I die.

On the flip side, there are some moral lines I won't cross, even if they sell—not because I'm judging but because that UF does nothing for me. For example, I get why a spoiled rich fixer-upper heroine is yummy for some. But for me, that character's a certain kind of woman I really did not like in college. I choose not to write this character. Ever.

And as much as I adore a hot sex scene, I always advise writers who don't feel comfortable writing hot to avoid doing so if that's not their thing.

So moral to taste.

If certain market trends make you squeamish, leave them alone.

But if you have a naughty fantasy, don't dismiss or fear it. Trust yourself and your audience. It could be your next big seller!

And that's as good of a segue as any into our next rule.

RULE 5:
Don't forget to butter up that sex

When you write cisgender male-female sex, think about the specifics of why this feels good for your female character on a Universal Fantasy level.

Personally, I am tired at the end of the day. So I like a sex scene where the guy is really into it and the woman doesn't have to do anything but lie back, enjoy his efforts, and come really hard. If she's tied up and unable to move, even better.

Most basic porn scenarios wouldn't turn me on. Even when I'm bored with nothing to do, I don't fantasize about getting into at least ten positions with the pizza boy. And I have no interest in watching a 20-minute blow job unless there's a weird power dynamic involved.

But a billionaire who

- yanks you out of your boring life,
- treats you to sumptuous Instagram-worthy meals you don't have to cook,
- takes you on shopping sprees for clothes and luxury items you could never afford on your own, and
- forces you to endure sensual massages that induce multiple orgasms?

Now we're talking!

There's also UF butter to be found in…

Gamified Sex (you're told not to come yet, tied up, blindfolded, etc.): This fantasy taps into our love of games.

Deal Sex (sex in exchange for something else, sex as payment, etc.): This fantasy stays controversial and *popular*. It would require more psychological and sociological depth than I have to explain why, but trust, it will always sell.

Instructional Sex (sex someone has to be guided or coached through): This especially applies to virginal sex. I'd argue readers don't adore this because of the heroine's purity—it's getting to watch her discover awesome sex.

And as I said above, this fantasy makes for fantastic oleo. If you write an over-40 divorcee who's been cruelly dumped by her selfish husband and gets to experience great sex for the first time, Imma read that book. Speaking of which…

Opposite Ex Sex (sex with someone who is the opposite of your ex): This is one of those real-life crossover fantasies. Readers can't resist when someone who's been treated cruelly and unfairly by an ex gets the exact opposite in a love interest.

Punishment sex (spankings for brats, uh-oh you came too early, etc.): You've been a bad girl and now you must deal with the consequences. Many of us were raised with strict rules and moral codes, and this kind of sex strums a pleasurable naughty chord inside of us.

Rough, and/or Dirty Talk Sex (you're dominated and told outrageous things until you come all over his dick. Good girl.): The cruel bully really likes you; the reserved CEO becomes a total ANIMAL when he's inside you; the shifter can't hold himself back when he meets you, his true mate—so many UFs work well with this kind of sex.

Confessional Sex (a big confession comes before, during, or after great sex): Trap voice is back to yell **Secret! Secret! Secret! Sex! Sex! Sex! Dopamine! Dopamine! Dopamine!**

. . .

Spotlight Sex (all attention on you, hero(es) interested in nothing but making you come): This is the opposite of male-centered porn. Honestly, you could probably write a great sex scene by doing the exact opposite of a typical porn setup.

Instead of leaving his neglected lover at home to give the plumber a twenty-minute blowjob then get in ten different positions, a businessman with a huge mansion…

- neglects work to eat out his love interest for as long as it takes for her to come in the morning
- instead of not touching her clit once—I've seen this happen so often in male-centered porn. Don't even get me started on finger banging)—he uses his huge rod and muscles to angle her at a position where her clit is constantly stimulated
- he applies steady pressure and pleasure by *not* changing positions until she comes again, and THEN
- he comes. Not because of her crazy gymnastics or plastic looks but simply because he achieved the ultimate goal of making her come.

And then there's my absolute favorite sex of all time…

Hate Sex (you two are just so mad at each other that you either have to physically fight or fuck—and yay for us readers, you choose fuck): This is one of those vanilla ice cream fantasies that never fails for me. Fantasizing about heroes and villains fucking instead of fighting is pretty much the only way I get through Marvel films—now that's a *What If* series many viewers would actually enjoy!

CHAPTER SEVENTEEN
UF FOR LIFE AND CAREER:
TROUBLESHOOTING UF FOR THE REST
OF YOUR LIFE AND CAREER

Okay, well, we're almost done with this book. And so far, we've discovered and explored Universal Fantasy. We've mined some of our favorite reads, movies, and shows for their audience-attracting gold. And we've learned how to market, outline, and write using Universal Fantasy butter to make your stories that much tastier.

Truly, you have everything you need to make the entire process of writing and selling stories way easier and delicious.

But here are a few more pieces of advice before you leave…

Some UF fantasies will sell better than others.

I'm super happy that most of my books hit the Kindle Store's Top 100 now that I've figured out Universal Fantasy. But I'll admit that every so once in a while—the winter holidays in particular—I release something just because I love it even though it doesn't have much butter.

Nobody:

Nobody:

Me at the beginning of 2021: Here's series 2 of my odd 12 Days of Christmas serial revolving around the romantic lives of Santa's elves. Happy Holidays!

Of course, that collected serial didn't make it anywhere near the Top 100, even though I'd discovered the power of Universal Fantasy by then. And that was totally alright. I knew that my elves weren't UF butter going in, and that helped me make great decisions around how to leverage this off-brand thing I simply wanted to write.

I didn't bother with a huge marketing campaign for it. I used the serial as a newsletter-only exclusive for the end of 2020. My readers could read the series for free when they signed up for my mailing list, or they could buy the collected serial on any platform between Jan. 10th and February 14th. The second serial became a huge success in its own way—by attracting thousands of readers to my newsletter.

On the flip side, I'm still occasionally surprised by a huge bestseller.

Since I began drafting this book, I've had to update my introduction because one of my novels made it into the top ten for the entire Kindle Store! So far in 2021, I've had a less-than-stellar debut and a wildly successful new release.

The difference now is that neither of those things caused me anxiety or confusion.

Big hugs to all my new newsletter subscribers. And as for the book that hit the top 10 in the Kindle Store—it was easy to figure out why it did and to replicate it if I so choose.

Which is why…

You should never stop mining for UF gold.

The number one exclamatory message I receive after my workshops is THANK YOU.

Number 2?

Some version of

"OMG, Theodora. Now that I've learned about Universal Fantasy, I see it EVERYWHERE."

Good!

Always be on the lookout for Universal Fantasy. Don't ever thoughtlessly consume entertainment.

Pay attention to EVERYTHING and figure out why it connects the way it does with audiences.

Even though I'm no longer a radio writer, I adore listening to new music. Why? The UFs, man! The UFs! Identifying the Universal Fantasies in Top 40 hits has become one of my favorite pastimes. Some songs have great beats, but the *best*, most popular songs trigger Universal Fantasies such as your ex regretting losing a great person like you, your love appreciating you above all others, or your haters watching you overcome and achieve your goals. The list goes on and on.

And believe me, getting real curious about why a particular song connects with audiences makes it way easier to listen to music you don't like. Speaking of which…

Don't hate on popular entertainment. It's okay to not like a book or show, but you should never get so busy griping about its very existence that you become confused about why it sells.

Actually, this is a great way to watch, read, and live in general. Instead of judging, try to understand the audience for every entertainment you encounter. **Understand each audience's wants and desires and how they manifest**. Break down Universal Fantasies everywhere you go.

On the flip side, **if you're stuck watching or reading a true dud, use my favorite thing to do in that situation: mind-edit the property**. What kind of Universal Fantasy would have made this premise and characters enjoyable for audiences?

Trust me, you'll appreciate having honed this skill when it's time to edit your own work.

Also, **don't practice Universal Fantasy just at home**. It doesn't matter what genre you're writing in or what kind of entertainment you prefer, occasionally consume things outside of them.

Look beyond your culture and borders. I love anime, Asian dramas, and in particular, hentai. These media mine a lot of Universal Fantasy gold that differs from what we see in mass entertainment in North America.

In general, try to add things outside of your own country's fare to your entertainment options to see what sparks on a global level. I always say that if it made it all the way to my American Netflix account, there's got to be some UF gold to be mined in them hills.

Also, **look to the past**. I low-key hated having to slog through all the dead white men books for my English literature Bachelor of Arts. But I adore that I recognized that the Angel character in *Buffy the Vampire Slayer* is full of Faustian motifs thanks to that degree.

But most of all…

Make your own Universal Fantasy list

Non-romance writers might have noticed that this entire book is super heavy on relationship, sex, and love UFs.

All, I can say after reading so many so-called general craft books that revolved completely around literary and sci-fi examples—most not even bothering to mention relationships, sex, or romance at all—is *you're welcome*! Hopefully, any non-romance writers come away from this book with a thorough understanding of how to add these three elements to their stories.

But seriously, I'm concerned that I've overwhelmed you with all of the UFs I've presented in this book. However, I'm assuming I haven't because I've extended the length of this workshop twice, and what's the No. 1 question I get after I'm done talking? "Do you have a list?"

Up until this book, my answer has always been "No, you should make your own."

And I'm still sticking with at least part of that answer here.

While there will be a quick reference at the end of this book, it is certainly not exhaustive, and I would super encourage you to make your own list. Especially if love stories aren't your thing.

Even if you're a romance writer like me, I'm sure my universal audience isn't your universal audience. My universal audience likes dark lava cake oozing with caramel and fudge and a scoop of vanilla ice cream on top.

But that might be too decadent for *your* universal audience. Your universal audience might like banana bread with just a pat of butter and a cozy cup of tea.

Both dishes require butter, but only one will be the best Universal Fantasy for your readers. Main point: The glossary is there for you but make your own list too.

And always remember…

Universal Fantasy is a GREAT tool, but it isn't the ONLY tool.

Keep in mind that the best way to produce bestsellers is by doing what the brilliant Allie Brosh refers to in *Hyperbole and a Half* as ALL THE THINGS:

- attend to craft
- write in series
- be super consistent with new releases
- write more books if you can
- make sure you have stellar editing and awesome covers
- plan out your marketing campaigns
- oh my gosh, take those life-changing ad classes (if you're wondering about the one I took—it was Skye Warren's. Sign up for her Author Thoughts newsletter to get a heads up the next time she offers it.)
- Newsletter, Social Media
- -DO ALL THE NUTRITIOUS THINGS

Mining for Universal Fantasy is an AWESOME tool, especially when you're stuck or outlining a new book.

But it should only be one of many in your writing toolbox. The better you are at craft and all the other stuff, the better Universal Fantasy will work for you.

CHAPTER EIGHTEEN
GOOD-BYE TO ME FOR NOW; HELLO TO UF FOREVER

Dearest Fellow Storytellers,

If you've made it to this point, Universal Fantasy is swirling like a blizzard in your head. For a while it will buzz loudly in the background, and you'll see it in everything you read, watch, and listen to—it might even come up in conversations!

When your friend calls to ask if she should "on again" with her boyfriend because maybe he's changed this time—that's a fantasy. (One of the ones that tend to work out better in books than real life).

You'll see the Slay-All-Day WonderGoddesses all over Instagram and wipe tears from your eyes during the vows at any True Love Match weddings you're invited to attend.

THE NEWBIE will confidently write her first book, so happy that she can point to one thing her future audience will enjoy in every scene. If she's traditional, she'll have a way easier time crafting a pitch letter that attracts an agent or publisher. If she's an indie author, look out buttery, irresistible book description—here she comes!

THE GAMBLER will write books with more confidence and will be able to budget for marketing big-hit books before he releases them.

THE ABANDONER will either happily let those past projects go—zombies can't be saved—OR she'll look at them with fresh eyes and grease them up with some UF butter.

THE BLANK will break down Side Character X's universal appeal and use that as the perfect hopping off point to figure out what one to three Universal Fantasies will serve their story best.

THE ENTERTAINER will cackle like a wizard as he joyfully writes certain buttery scenes because he *knows* his readers are going to freaking GOBBLE THEM UP.

THE GRIZZLED HEART will sit down at her computer, and for the first time in years, she'll see them. The people around her fire. Waiting to hear her story.

No matter what kind of writer you are, Universal Fantasy is here to serve you now—as happily as enchanted dishware in a castle.

And don't worry about that loud buzz—it will eventually quiet down into a steady hum in the background. Like a Chrome Extension you can use or not use, it's up to you. Butter to taste.

No matter what, thank you for being a storyteller.

There are readers escaping into our stories right now because they're stuck inside or upset with what's going on in the real world or trying to deal with the heartbreak of losing a loved one.

Our stories are there for them in their darkest hours. And when they simply need a break.

So, thank you! Thank you for volunteering to stand up at the fire and tell your tale.

Keep up the amazing work.

So much love (and fantasy),

Theodora

P. S. Good-bye for now, but if you want to stay in touch with me, please sign up for my newsletter at 7figurefiction.substack.com. I'll send you my list of the **Top Six Reasons Your Book Isn't Selling—and How UF Can Fix Them**. And when crazy delicious shows, movies, and books hit the zeitgeist, believe me, I'm going to break those delicious tales down for you!

QUICK REFERENCE
FOR THE UNIVERSAL FANTASIES MENTIONED IN THIS BOOK

(friendly reminder: make your own too!)

AIR HE BREATHES, THE by Brittany Cherry

- Two widowed and suffering people heal come back and fix each other with love

DISNEY'S *BEAUTY AND THE BEAST*

- Removal from boring life (also, *Keeping Lily* by Izzy Sweet and Sean Moriarty, *Her Viking Wolf* by Theodora Taylor)
- Surprise! The bully really likes you!
- Reverse Bully. He's a bully to everybody else, but a teddy bear for you (*PHANTOM: Her Ruthless Fiancé* by Theodora Taylor)
- Abuse of power. Bosshole.
- The most popular/wealthiest guy in [insert place] chooses you (also, *Twilight, Pride and Prejudice*)

- Servants who are delighted to serve (also, J.R. Ward's *doggens*)
- Fixer-Upper
- Wounded MC in need of healing love
- Not just any gift, THE RIGHT GIFT
- Love triangle or whatever shape you want. More than one person wants you. (also, *Titanic, Hunger Games* by Suzanne Collins, *Vampire Diaries*)
- A really, really good MAKEOVER (also, *My Fair Lady, Karate Kid*)
- Banging a beast

BRIDGERTON

- Opposite World from Yours (also, *The Lion, the Witch, and the Wardrobe, Alice in Wonderland, The Wizard of Oz, Harry Potter, Moana*)
- Nightmare World (*Hunger Games, The Walking Dead, Three-Body Problem* trilogy by Cixin Liu)
- Inclusion for the WIN (also, *Hamilton, Hollywood, A Court of Thorns and Roses* by Sarah J. Maas, *The Kiss Quotient* by Helen Hoang)
- Rules, Scandal, Secrets, and Questions (also, *Games of Thrones*)

CINDERELLA

- Instalove that you don't have to work for
- True Love Match (also, *Long Shot* by Kennedy Ryan
- Suffering MC (also, *Lover Eternal* by J.R. Ward, *Ten Count* by Rihito Takarai)
- Obsessed Prince
- Badass Cinderella

- Pluck Rewarded. #PrincessPersisted (also, *The Martian* by Andy Weir)

COLOR PURPLE, THE

- Siblings reunited (also, *This is Us*)
- Being serenaded by someone who can really sing. (also, *Schitt's Creek*)
- Parent's forgiveness

GREY'S ANATOMY

- That one night stand is THE ONE (and also your new boss)
- Racers, start your engines… [Competition Avatar Butter]
- Comeback kids [Dropping Your Character's Ice Cream to Set Them Up for a UF]
- Overcoming your parental privilege

PESTILENCE by Lauren Thalassa

- Saving someone you love
- Formidable Villain Hero (also, *Terminator*)
- Supernatural Bully
- The Power of the Magical Pussy

QUEEN'S GAMBIT, THE

- Getting really good at chess.
- Earning a mother's approval through your talent and making a few of that parent's dreams come true.
- Slay-All-Day vintage wardrobe.
- Opposite World...of [insert unusual sport]. (also, *Fence* by C.S. Pascat)
- A *woman* gets a karate kid makeover in a classically male sport
- All your exes happily work together for your benefit.

SCANDAL

- Faithful Dog protects, loves, and attacks for you unconditionally (also, *The Expanse, Brooklyn 9-9*)
- Slay-All-Day WonderGoddess (also, *Shopaholic* by Sophie Kinsella, Carrie from *Sex in the City*, Elektra from *Pose*, and Beyoncé video albums)
- The most powerful man in your story world is obsessed with you
- Created Families

BOOKS BY THEODORA TAYLOR

GOLDIE AND THE THREE BEARS

- Shelter from the storm/cold
- Familiar fairytale retold

HIS TO CLAIM (with Eve Vaughn as Taylor Vaughn)

- Banging an alien beast
- Getting punished because you've been bad
- A Formidable Villain Hero
- Abuse of Power

HOLT: Her Ruthless Billionaire

- Opposite sides of the tracks first love.
- Bitter and/or tragic breakup.
- Single Dad with out-of-control kid
- Punishment disguised as a job.
- Heroine has a HUGE SECRET that compels her to make an *indecent proposal deal*

VICTOR: Her Ruthless Crush

- Low self-esteem, plus-sized relatable character
- Fish-out-of-International water
- Interesting talent
- Dangerous and violent hero willing to do evil things to help an protect
- Teen who commands adults
- Cold and Harsh Anti-Hero meets someone warm and loving

RANDOM UFs

- The reader gets to say "I was RIGHT!"

- The "Just as I Am" heroine is super relatable butter (*Bridgit Jones Diary*, *Crazy Ex-Girlfriend*, and any Mindy Kaling show)

- **Oleo fantasies** uses the UF energy from one genre for a totally opposite category (ex. Age gap UF butter for same age over-40s romance, Ruby Dixon's small town series—set on a harsh planet with huge blue aliens (*Ice Planet Barbarians*), *The Good Place*)

- Universal Fantasies borne out of social justice or frustrations with the real world are GOLD.

- SEX BUTTER!!!

Still not enough UF for ya? Sign up for my newsletter at 7figurefiction.substack.com to keep the Universal Fantasies coming!

ALSO BY THEODORA TAYLOR

ALPHA KINGS

Her Viking Wolf

Wolf and Punishment

Wolf and Prejudice

Wolf and Soul

Her Viking Wolves

ALPHA FUTURE

Her Dragon Everlasting

NAGO: Her Forever Wolf

KNUD: Her Big Bad Wolf

RAFES: Her Fated Wolf

Her Dragon Captor

Her Dragon King

ALIEN OVERLORDS (as Taylor Vaughn)

His to Claim

His to Steal

His to Keep

THE SCOTTISH WOLVES

Her Scottish Wolf

Her Scottish King

Her Scottish Warrior

RUTHLESS TYCOONS

HOLT: Her Ruthless Scion

HOLT: Her Ruthless Billionaire

ZAHIR: Her Ruthless Sheikh

LUCA: Her Ruthless Don

AMBER: His to Reclaim

RUTHLESS TYCOONS: Broken and Ruthless

KEANE: Her Ruthless Ex

STONE: Her Ruthless Enforcer

RASHID: Her Ruthless Boss

RUTHLESS TRIAD

VICTOR: Her Ruthless Crush

VICTOR: Her Ruthless Owner

VICTOR: Her Ruthless Husband

HAN: Her Ruthless Mistake

PHANTOM: Her Ruthless Fiancé

RUTHLESS FAIRYTALES

Cynda and the City Doctor

Billie and the Russian Beast

Goldie and the Three Bears

Reina and the Heavy Metal Prince

(newsletter exclusive)

THE VERY BAD FAIRGOODS

His for Keeps

His Forbidden Bride

His to Own

RUTHLESS MC

WAYLON: Amira and the Grumpy Reaper

GRIFFIN: Red and the Big Bad Reaper

REAPERS: Dr. Snow and the Vengeful Reapers

HADES: Stephanie and the Merciless Reaper

RUTHLESS BOSSES

His Pretend Baby

His Revenge Baby

His Enduring Love

His Everlasting Love

RUTHLESS BUSINESS

Her Ruthless Tycoon

Her Ruthless Cowboy

Her Ruthless Possessor

Her Ruthless Bully

RUTHLESS RUSSIANS

Her Russian Billionaire

Her Russian Surrender

Her Russian Beast

Her Russian Brute

HOT HARLEQUINS WITH HEART

Vegas Baby

Love's Gamble

ABOUT THE AUTHOR

After logging time as a music journalist, playwright, and radio writer, **Theodora Taylor** began writing hot books with heart in 2012. With forty plus romances published to date, she has earned five KDP All-Star bonuses. Known for writing alternative heroes and smart, feisty heroines, Theodora's *50 Loving States* series has become a one-click stop for an ever-growing number of rabid readers. When not thinking of ways to write and sell even more hot books with heart, she enjoys spending time with her amazing family, going on date nights with her wonderful husband, learning German, watching ALL the Shonda Rhimes shows ever, and attending parties thrown by others. She also loves hearing from voices that don't originate inside her head, so please…

Follow TT on Instagram
https://www.instagram.com/taylor.theodora/

Sign for up for TT's Substak
https://7figurefiction.substack.com/